Mastering Council Meetings

A guidebook for elected officials and local governments

Mastering
Council Meetings

A guidebook for elected officials and local governments

by Ann G. Macfarlane, PRP, CAE
and Andrew L. Estep, CAE

Jurassic Parliament

Mastering Council Meetings:
A guidebook for elected officials and local governments

First edition 2013
ISBN-13: 978-1482708189
LCCN: 2013904640
PRINTED IN THE UNITED STATES OF AMERICA
10 9 8 7 6 5 4 3 2 1

Jurassic Parliament

Bad meetings drive us crazy.
Welcome to the sanity of
Robert's Rules as presented
by Jurassic Parliament.

Table of Contents

Mastering Council Meetings

Preface

In our society, managing discussion and public comment can be a challenge for leaders of elected governing bodies and citizen advisory groups. This book offers principles, rules and insights that create the conditions for efficient, fair and productive discussion, effective decision-making and orderly public comment at council meetings. All content is based on *Robert's Rules of Order Newly Revised, 11th edition*, also referred to as "Robert." (See Appendix A for information about all the books we refer to in this work.)

Of course, information is only useful when applied in practice. Running a meeting of a public body is a learned performance skill. It requires certain habits and turns of phrase which do not come naturally. Anyone planning to run such a meeting should accept the fact that "mistakes will be made" and resolve not to mind it. With time and practice, the presider will get better, as will the meetings.

Members of councils as well as mayors, chairs and presidents will benefit from learning this content and bringing it to their meetings.

For the sake of simplicity, the word "council" as used in this book also refers to boards, commissions, committees, or any public governing body or citizen advisory group.

Failure is not fatal. It is the courage to continue that counts.

Winston Churchill

About This Book

This book is intended both to be instructional and to serve as a resource. We encourage you to read it through with highlighter and sticky notes at hand. We hope that you will return to it again and again.

You may note that occasionally the same point is made more than once—this is deliberate. We want to ensure that the reader has easy access to key information in tough situations as the need arises.

We also sometimes refer to the rules for private organizations in order to put the requirements for meetings of elected officials and public bodies into the broader context of parliamentary procedure.

While we make occasional reference to laws and regulations, please note that we are not attorneys. The purpose of this book is solely to provide general education and information about council and public meetings. The reader is advised to seek a qualified professional for guidance in specific situations.

ACCORDING TO ROBERT

Throughout this book quotes are given from Robert's Rules of Order Newly Revised, *11th edition. These quotes are in this format preceded by the heading "According to Robert" and ending with a page number.*

IN OUR EXPERIENCE

We also offer up anecdotes drawn from our personal adventures with nonprofit boards, meetings and Robert's Rules of Order. These anecdotes are intentional diversions from the topic at hand, alleviating the tedium inherent in material of this kind.   —Andrew

About the Authors

The authors of this book are business colleagues in Seattle, Washington, who met through their involvement in managing professional associations. A few words from each:

Ann Macfarlane

I began my career as a diplomat with the U.S. Foreign Service serving in Lahore, Pakistan. Later I became a Russian-to-English translator and was elected president of the American Translators Association. Wanting to do a good job at running our board meetings, I took up *Robert's Rules of Order Newly Revised*, but found the book to be impenetrable, confusing and boring—it's more than 800 pages long!

I would have given up, but our bylaws, like the bylaws of 90% of the voluntary associations in this country, said, "Meetings shall be run according to *Robert's Rules of Order Newly Revised*, latest edition." I kept on reading and studying, and eventually realized that there is a core to Robert's Rules that is vital to fair and effective meetings, wrapped in a lot of verbiage and complexity that is not essential.

From that beginning I developed Jurassic Parliament as a way of cutting through the confusion of procedure and jargon, making the core principles of Robert's Rules available to everyone. I used my experience as a diplomat and a translator to find ways to extract the essence of this method of meeting management and decision-making. In this book Andrew and I offer our readers what we consider to be the best of Robert's Rules—a commonsense and down-to-earth approach. We've seen amazing results when this method is applied, in many differing types of organizations. (See our website, www.jurassicparliament.com, and search for "Success Stories" to learn more.) We can help you turn painful meetings into productive, pleasant and effective events that get the work of your organization done.

Andrew Estep

Like many in my generation who felt lost out of high school and at a loss about college, I enlisted in the U.S. Air Force. There I learned many of life's lessons that continue to serve me well: the value of service to my country and my fellow, the importance of good organization to accomplishing goals and how communication is the key to all effective human interaction.

With the end of the Cold War, my career in aerospace ended and I was drawn to nonprofit work. A short stint in health care led me to work in association management as the executive director of a regional organization. There a group of patient and compassionate association executives, my colleagues at the time, showed me the value of the human factor. I learned it is not enough to have efficient and effective systems; one must also account for and celebrate the diversity and strength that people bring to these systems.

In 2001, I bought an association management company, put everything I had learned to use and discovered it was not enough. I also had to learn the value of compromise and collaboration, and how to maintain many different systems in varied milieu. In other words, I learned to juggle.

Thankfully, I met my friend and colleague, Ann Macfarlane, in 2004. In 2007 we became business partners and began working together on Jurassic Parliament. Ann taught me the value of Robert's Rules of Order and proper parliamentary procedure. Since then we have refined our training and information services to better serve our greater community.

Mastering Council Meetings is a distillation of our work together. We believe that as you implement the systems and methods outlined here your city or county council will be transformed. We challenge you to conduct your meetings "According to Robert."

Why the Dinosaurs?

People often ask how the dinosaurs became a part of Jurassic Parliament. It all goes back to 1999 when, as Ann described, she was newly elected as president of the American Translators Association. She struggled with Robert but gradually began to get a sense of how the system worked. She wanted to share it with her colleagues on the board of directors, but wasn't sure how to do that without boring them silly.

One concept that came to her was the realization that a "motion" is not just words, it is a thing. Once a group has made a main motion and started discussing it, they have to dispose of it in some way—to adopt it, defeat it, send it off to a committee—but they can't just abandon it. She was mulling over how to get this idea across when her eye fell on some Jurassic Park dinosaurs belonging to her 9-year-old son, Steve. The movie was very popular at that time, and the house had lots of those critters underfoot.

Ann picked up a T-rex and thought, "This could be the main motion— it certainly is a definite 'thing'—and then we could use the dimetrodon for the amendment, another 'thing,' and show that the dimetrodon blocks the forward progress of the T-rex. You have to vote on the amendment before the main motion can move ahead...and a 'point of order' could be a flying dinosaur that soars over the heads of the other motions..."

From that moment she developed the whole system for showing how motions work in the city of Dinopolis, which has given a lot of pleasure in teaching a subject that can be perceived as dull. She owes it all to Steven Spielberg and her son Steve.

Introduction

Introduction

Our democratic culture, and this book, assumes that all group members have equal rights and an equal voice. We also assume that these rights change when an individual assumes a specific role within a group. It is important to have a clear understanding of how these rights change and why.

The achievements of an organization are the results of the combined effort of each individual.

Vince Lombardi

Two Types of Organization

In learning to master meetings of public bodies, it is vital to understand the difference between two types of organizations.

An "accountability hierarchy" is shaped like a pyramid or triangle. The person at the top is "the boss." This person selects people to do the work of the organization, directs them in their task, gives them feedback and, if they do not perform adequately, fires them. We are all very familiar with this structure, since it occurs in virtually every business corporation, in the military and in many other human institutions.

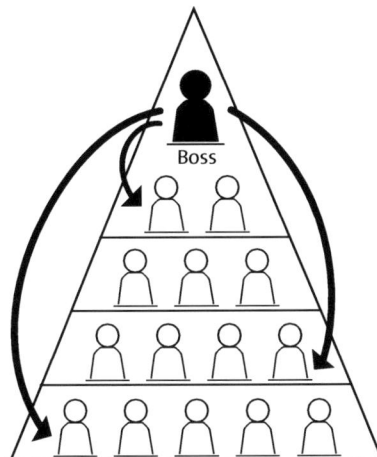

Figure 1. Accountability Hierarchy

A "voluntary association" has an entirely different structure. This type of organization is shaped like a circle. A group of people come together to achieve a common purpose, set up some rules for themselves and choose a leader. All the members have equal standing and, in general, one vote. The leader's role here is very different—she must convince the members by persuasion, not direct them by giving orders. She is a facilitator, not "the boss."

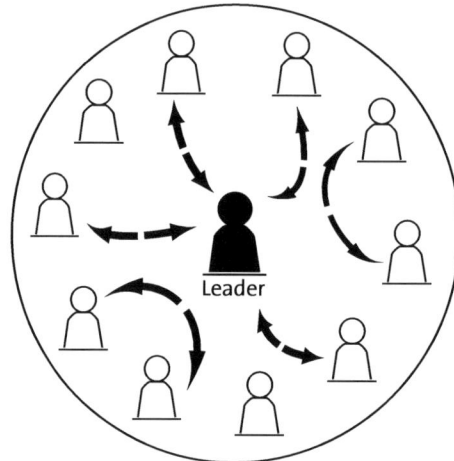

Figure 2. Voluntary Association

A city council is a voluntary association whose members are elected by the people. Robert's Rules of Order were created for just such voluntary associations.

Nature of a Governing Board

The Standard Code of Parliamentary Procedure, another significant authority on meetings, makes the following important point about the nature of a governing board:

> *All members of a governing board share in a joint and collective authority which exists and can be exercised only when the group is in session.*

This is why meeting procedure is so critical—a group must make the most of the time it spends together, because that is when its authority can be exercised.

Who's in charge?

It is important to know the source of the authority by which a body makes decisions. A city council or municipal governing board is subject to the laws of the state in which it is established, and to any federal laws that apply. A board, commission or committee is subject to the city council (or other body) that appoints it, and to the ordinances and regulations of the jurisdiction in which it is established.

Even if a state does not give explicit authority to city councils or your body to create such rules, the courts have found that governmental bodies are subject to "common parliamentary law." In other words, people cannot just do what they like—they must observe common standards of fair process and behavior. Robert's Rules of Order is accepted by many as the definitive statement of common parliamentary law.

Levels of authority

It is helpful to visualize the different sources of authority for the actions of a city council or other body in a hierarchy like the one below. Each lower level of this ranking must conform with the requirements of the higher levels. For example, if state law prohibits a mayor from voting whenever money is involved, the council rules of procedure cannot allow the mayor to cast a vote about the budget.

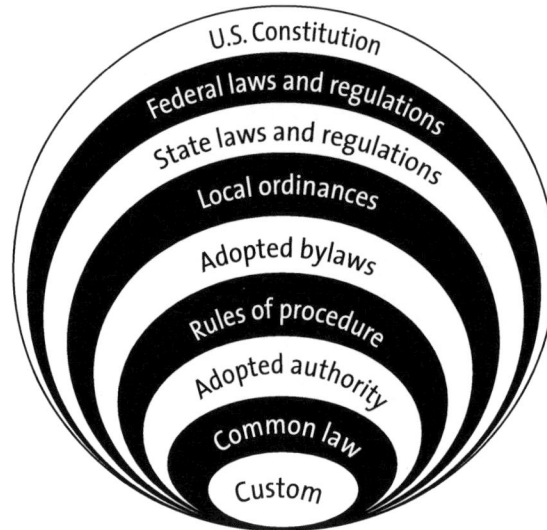

Figure 3. Levels of Authority

1. U.S. Constitution
2. Federal laws and regulations (if any)
3. State laws and regulations
4. Local ordinances (if any)
5. Bylaws adopted by body (if any)
6. Rules of procedure adopted by body (if any)
7. Adopted parliamentary authority if any (Robert's Rules, The Standard Code, or others)
8. Common parliamentary law
9. Custom

Should our council adopt Robert's Rules of Order?

Some councils have adopted, by resolution or ordinance, a set of meeting guidelines, and others have not. Many of these guidelines include reference to Robert's Rules of Order, using such language as "meetings shall be governed by Robert's Rules of Order and these council rules of procedure. In case of a conflict, the council rules of procedure shall prevail."

It has at times been suggested that Robert's Rules is too complicated for small cities and towns, and they would do better not to adopt it. The book is complicated, but it still provides the best and most useful set of rules of order for civic bodies—provided that folks are willing to do a little work and learn how to use Robert's Rules properly.

The use of written motions and amendments provides an efficient and fair way to consider proposals and modify them in accord with the group's preferences. The method is a little unusual, in that amendments are taken up before the motion is voted on, but once groups get used to it, the system works well.

The rule that no one may speak a second time until everyone who wishes to do so has spoken once is vital to equalizing power imbalances and giving everyone a fair shake in discussion. It should be observed by all groups, whether or not they have formally adopted Robert's Rules.

Robert's Rules provides "special rules for small boards" that can be useful for councils, should they choose to apply them. It also allows groups to develop and apply their own "special rules of order," so if a body wishes to change something, it is perfectly free to do so. These rules may also be called "standing rules."

In sticky situations, "do-it-yourself" rulemaking can lead to ad hoc invention of rules by the mayor or council president. A presider who makes up rules or improvises on the basis of vague memories from student government days is a sure path to problems, especially if the rule-maker has an air of authority.

While councils often rely on their attorney for advice in this arena, few attorneys have had serious training in parliamentary procedure and few correct the common and widespread misunderstandings about Robert's Rules.

A body cannot do its work without some procedural guidelines. Failing to adopt Robert's Rules does not mean that there are no guidelines—but without a specific "parliamentary authority" in times of conflict, a group will be driven back to rely on "common parliamentary law."

Finding out what "common parliamentary law" requires and how it applies to a given situation is likely to be complicated and expensive, requiring time and attention from legal counsel and qualified parliamentary consultants. Far better to have set the terms of discourse in advance, so that everyone knows and agrees to the way they will consider matters.

IN OUR EXPERIENCE

Avoid the imposters! By "Robert's Rules" we mean Robert's Rules of Order Newly Revised, 11th edition. *Other books purport to be as good as Robert, but none have the depth and authority of the original Robert. Also, all out-of-date editions should be tossed in the recycling bin, not used.*   —Andrew

Adopting a set of commonsense guidelines based on Robert's Rules, incorporating it by reference for the more unusual or complicated situations that may arise, and then committing to the education necessary to get everyone on the same page, will pay big dividends for every council willing to make the effort.

We recommend that every city council and government provide a copy of *Robert's Rules of Order Newly Revised in Brief* to each council member. This little book is a splendid summary of the rules applicable to all but the most exceptional situations. It is value-priced, and it can be read in an evening.

Note, however, that *Robert's Rules of Order Newly Revised in Brief* may not be adopted as an authority in its own right. It functions as a signpost to the "big book," *Robert's Rules of Order Newly Revised, 11th edition.* We believe that mayors, presidents, clerks, secretaries and anyone wishing to delve more deeply will find it beneficial to purchase this book. Having the authoritative Robert at one's fingertips is essential for good process, and for personal confidence. The spiral-bound version offered by the National Association of Parliamentarians is easy to work with and annotate because it lies flat on the table.

Part I
Fundamentals

Part I: Fundamentals

As in all things, a clear and common understanding of the fundamentals can dramatically impact effectiveness. For council meetings, these fundamentals include the role and function of the presider, the nature and types of meetings, and voting's permutations. In Part I we explain:

- The role of the presider;
- The components and types of meetings;
- How agendas and minutes function; and
- The basics of voting.

Presiding

When running a meeting, the presider is both the most important person in the room and the least important person in the room. The ability to keep things in hand while maintaining this paradox is crucial to successful meetings.

Different people with different personalities will display different styles, but there are certain habits that make for a more effective presider. These additional steps will help in developing a strong presiding style:

A presider should always use the pronoun "our" rather than the pronoun "my" in referring to the council, its activities or its members. Always say, "I'll ask our city clerk" rather than "I'll ask my clerk." To use the pronoun "my" and "mine" means that you are reducing people, organizations and entities to a part of yourself. The staff, the resources and the city belong to everyone, not to the mayor or the presider.

A leader is best when people barely know he exists, when his work is done, his aim fulfilled, they will say: we did it ourselves.

Lao Tzu

Cultivate an attitude that is warm, calm and in control. Connect with people as a colleague and a fellow human, while maintaining the authority of the position.

Formality is a friend. Use titles rather than first names. Do not try to be chummy.

Ideally, no one should be able to tell whom the chair likes or dislikes. Strive to treat everyone with fairness, no matter your personal feelings.

Cultivate the ability to observe yourself with "the third eye," to step back and notice when your voice becomes shrill, your temper rises or you are in danger of losing your cool. Know your own weaknesses and take steps to counterbalance them.

When another person is speaking, listen to her as if there were no one else in the room. The undivided attention of the presider will assure each person that their concerns are taken seriously and that they are respected. (Council members should do this too.)

Take the time to memorize the language of the presider so that you can speak with confidence, and control the ebb and flow of meeting discussion. See "Addressing Disorder" on page 101 for specific examples.

Do not be afraid to admit ignorance or confusion. When in doubt, propose a course of action to the group and let the group decide.

Above all else, remain the servant of the group. The presider's job is to help the group make up its mind. As long as you keep to this role, you will be fulfilling your duty.

Effective listening is a professional achievement—achieved only through hard work.

Tom Peters

Duties

Newly elected mayors are sometimes expected to start running their meetings with little or no training in meeting procedure. Instead, it is assumed that they have "picked it up" as they attended earlier meetings of the group. While experience teaches much, a little study can make a large difference and produce far better meetings.

A mayor, as meeting presider, is given these duties by parliamentary law. Keep the following list, taken from Robert (pp. 449-450), handy. It is important to know what these responsibilities are, and what they are not. Above all, the presider serves the group and assists it to make its own decisions. The mayor is the facilitator, not the dictator.

It is the presider's job to:

Duty	Description of duty
Open meeting	To open the meeting at the appointed time by taking the chair and calling the meeting to order, having ascertained that a quorum is present.
Announce next activity	To announce in proper sequence the next activity before the assembly in accordance with the prescribed order of business, agenda or program.
Recognize members	To recognize members who are entitled to the floor.
State questions and put to vote	To state and to put to vote all questions that legitimately come before the assembly as motions or that otherwise arise in the course of proceedings, and to announce the result of each vote; or, if a motion that is not in order is made, to rule it out of order.
Refuse to recognize dilatory motions	To protect the assembly from obviously dilatory (time-wasting) motions by refusing to recognize them.
Enforce order and decorum	To enforce the rules relating to debate and those relating to order and decorum within the assembly.
Expedite business	To expedite business in every way compatible with the rights of members.
Decide all questions of order	To decide all questions of order subject to appeal—unless, when in doubt, the presiding officer prefers initially to submit such a question to the assembly for decision.
Respond to inquiries	To respond to inquiries of members relating to parliamentary procedure or factual information bearing on the business of the assembly.
Authenticate documents	To authenticate by his or her signature, when necessary, all acts, orders and proceedings of the assembly.
Close meeting	To declare the meeting adjourned when the assembly so votes or—where applicable—at the time prescribed in the program, or at any time in the event of a sudden emergency affecting the safety of those present.

Striking a balance

One of the challenges that face newly elected mayors is knowing how much to speak at meetings. Many mayors are hard-charging individuals who are accustomed to influencing the course of events and are not shy about voicing opinions. It can be a challenge to adapt to the different requirements of running council meetings.

In a democratic system, the person who runs the meetings of a body of peers is not the boss. The presider is in charge of certain aspects of the meeting, such as making sure that the meeting is fair, and that everyone has an equal chance to speak. With regard to substance, though, the presider is the servant of the group. This role is to help the group make up its mind, to assist the group, rather than to tell the group what to do.

Robert's Rules of Order recognizes the temptation that a gavel presents to the presider. (The members also can be tempted to give undue weight or influence to the presider.) It specifies that ordinarily the person running the meeting does not take part in debate at all. The presider has the right to debate and vote, but refrains from exercising that right in order to remain impartial.

In a city council of no more than twelve members, the rules for "small boards" apply. Robert's Rules states that in a small board, the presider may participate in debate.

A mayor who is willing and able to hold back will serve her council better than one who waxes on and gives his opinion freely. It is not easy to distill the best course of action for a city council from among the many differing options, facts and opinions that must be considered. The mayor who speaks out at length becomes a factor in the debate. When refraining and earnestly, genuinely seeking to learn the opinions of others, the presider is more of a facilitator. The best practice is that even in smaller boards, a presider who chooses this role will help the organization more than one who is a full-contact participant.

Therefore, we suggest that mayors speak and debate last, after everyone has had a chance. This is a Jurassic Parliament position that differs from Robert's Rules. Besides making the mayor more impartial, this approach leaves room to sum up the debate, which can be critical in helping everyone see the big picture.

It is also essential that a city council follow the most neglected rule in all of Robert's Rules, the rule that no one may speak twice until everyone has had a chance to speak once. This includes the honorable mayor! By giving everyone a chance in turn, all voices are heard. The extroverts and old-timers are not allowed to dominate the discussion, and a better decision can be made for the good of the city.

The people to fear are not those who disagree with you, but those who disagree with you and are too cowardly to let you know.

Napoleon

Meetings

The key fact to remember when participating in a discussion at council, commission or committee meetings is that discussion in these settings is not a conversation. The fluid give and take of good conversation is one of life's joys. But a governing body meeting together is organized on very different principles from a group of friends or a family gathering. Being clear on this from the start will spare members many bad moments.

The hope in a governing body is that all will share thoughts and views, and that out of the discussion a collective wisdom will emerge. Under the right conditions, groups can make decisions that are much better than any individual would make. Under the wrong conditions, groups can make terrible decisions that take the body in the wrong direction. Groups can also get lost in a stagnant quagmire of mediocrity.

What are the right conditions? Every member must be free, and feel free, to express honest opinions about the subject being discussed. All too often in group discussions, members conceal their inner reservations, concerns or worries about a proposed course of action in order to be pleasant. They do not want to make waves, so they remain silent. This is deadly.

The best collective decisions are the product of disagreement and contest, not consensus and compromise.

James Surowiecki

In Our Experience

A volunteer body, council or board of directors that agrees all the time is doomed. Either the minority opinion is not being expressed or the group is not grappling with issues of sufficient import to properly lead the organization. Any group that has consistent unanimous votes needs to take a close look at itself to understand why this is the case, and take action to change. —Andrew

Another requirement is that every member should focus on the issues at hand. All too often members are present in the body but absent in spirit. They are "free riders," assuming that others have thought about the proposal and that they do not need to look at it closely, to ask questions or to probe for weaknesses. Active participation of everyone in the group is necessary to make good decisions.

Another requirement is the need for courtesy and respect. Due to the way the human brain works, groups whose members attack each other, who use rough language, who insult others or who question the motives of fellow members cannot make good decisions. The emotions and upset from such challenges interfere with the members' ability to think calmly and rationally. People cannot think straight when they are frightened or angry, so it is essential to establish respect and courtesy in all meetings.

The final requirement is a structure that will ensure fairness in discussion. Leaving everything to spontaneous conversation will mean that some people dominate the discussion and others are not heard. Structure is critical, and easy to achieve by knowing and applying a few simple rules. Robert's Rules of Order is a very linear system that provides this structure.

Sharing power is a critical part of getting people to take responsibility for their own futures.

Lawrence E. Suskind

Meeting principles

Principles for members

In order to achieve the right conditions, all members need to understand and act according to the basic principles of meetings. We like James Lochrie's formulation, which he has given us permission to use. It is excerpted from his book, *Meeting Procedure*:

- The majority must be allowed to rule.
- The minority have rights that must be respected.
- Members have a right to information to help make decisions.
- Courtesy and respect are required.
- All members have equal rights, privileges and obligations.
- Members have a right to an efficient meeting.

Principles for the presider

Jurassic Parliament has formulated some important additional principles:

- The presider, the person running the meeting, is both the most important person in the room and the least important person in the room.
- The presider must be strict on procedure—a benevolent dictator.
- The presider is not responsible for the decision the group makes.
- The presider must balance the emotional and procedural aspects of every meeting.

Flow of authority

These principles produce this flow of authority at a meeting:

1. The group adopts its rules and guidelines.
2. In attending, members accept the rules of the group.
3. During meetings, the presider applies the rules for the benefit of the group.
4. All persons present at a meeting have an obligation to obey the legitimate orders of the presider.
5. Any member who disagrees with a ruling, decision or order by the presider may appeal the ruling.
6. If another member seconds the appeal, the group will decide by majority vote whether the ruling, decision or order is legitimate.
7. The presider obeys the group's decision.

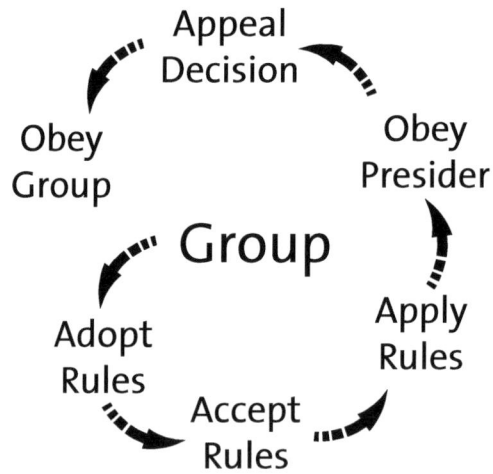

Figure 4. Flow of Authority

IN OUR EXPERIENCE

A set of council procedures that we were reviewing included the sentence, "All persons present at a meeting must obey the mayor's orders." This is a wild distortion of the principles that actually apply. If this language were in place, a mayor could say "Go pick up my laundry" and a citizen in attendance would be obliged to comply. It's no wonder that elected leaders sometimes get a swelled head when they are given this kind of license! As seen above, the correct parliamentary language is that attendees must obey "the legitimate orders of the presiding officer," which is quite a different proposition. —Ann

Notice requirements

The point of notice requirements is twofold: to ensure that some members don't pull a fast one on the others, and in the case of councils, to ensure that the public knows what is going on. Insufficient notice has sometimes been found by the courts to invalidate an entire meeting and its actions, so it is important to know what is required for your group. Your body may be required to give notice of your meetings in public newspapers, on the web and/or at the council chambers.

Note that if sufficient notice has not been given, state law may state that by showing up at a meeting, the member accepts the lack of notice (unless her sole purpose is to protest that adequate notice was not given).

Public bodies must comply with the notice requirements of their jurisdiction, which are different depending on the state, county or city involved. Notice requirements may vary by type of meeting.

SAMPLE NOTICE

Notice is hereby given that the Dinopolis City Council
will hold its regular meeting on
Monday, January 28, 2013 at 5:00 p.m.
in the City Council Chambers,
989 Port Street, First Floor, Dinopolis

The business before the meeting is given in the attached agenda and may also include any other such business as may be properly brought before the Council at such meeting. The City Council may take action to accept, reject or modify any or all proposed programs.

Citizens and residents are welcome to attend the meeting and to address the Council during the Public Comment session.

All materials pertaining to this meeting are available on the Dinopolis City Council website.

Anthony Ankylosaurus
City Clerk
City of Dinopolis

Meeting types

Meetings are the way a council, commission, committee or board does its work. They are the essential tool of our democratic society. We hope that these short descriptions will clear up some of the confusion that prevails about types of meetings.

Regular meetings

The ordinary, routine meeting that is scheduled once or twice a month or once a week is a "regular meeting." Customarily an ordinance or resolution will state that "the council will meet on the first and third Mondays" or something similar. (For a private organization, having such a rule is sufficient notice of the meeting.) Regular meetings are sometimes listed as "business meeting" or simply as "meeting."

Annual meetings

Membership organizations and boards of directors may have a requirement in their bylaws for an "annual meeting," which takes place once a year by definition. Usually this meeting is the right place for electing officers, adopting budgets, reporting to the membership or other special activities. We have not encountered an "annual meeting" for a city council, since public bodies usually meet rather frequently and have a regular schedule of business to cover.

Special meetings

A meeting that is called outside of the regular schedule would be a "special meeting." State regulation, council procedures and/or bylaws may specify who may call a "special meeting" and how much notice is required.

Executive session

"Executive session" is one customary term used to describe a secret or closed meeting. This type of meeting is open only to council members and, if desired, invited staff or guests. There are times in any organization when executive session is appropriate and necessary. Your state will likely limit the topics that may be discussed in executive session and may also limit what actions can be taken. Members are prohibited from disclosing the content of executive session. Minutes from executive sessions, if any, are approved during executive session and are kept separate from the minutes of regular sessions.

Study sessions

Many councils schedule "study sessions" or "work sessions" that provide the opportunity to explore problems or proposed legislation in greater depth, with staff input. Often it is stipulated that action may not be taken at a study session, and usually public comment is not allowed.

Committee of the Whole

This rather strange jargon term is used when a council or other body is meeting "as a committee"—usually, it is a type of study session. The whole group is considered to be a committee, which allows for greater informality, and sometimes a more conversational style of discussion. Final decisions may not be taken during a meeting of the Committee of the Whole.

Emergency meetings

State regulations may allow for emergency meetings, which can be called without observing the usual notice requirements. Sometimes fewer than usual members are present at an emergency meeting. If such is the case, it may be required that actions taken at an emergency meeting be "ratified" (approved) by the whole body at its next regular session—and if such approval were not given, the people who took the action would be individually liable for any ill consequences of their action.

Public hearings

Public hearings are held for the purpose of obtaining input from the public. They differ from the types of meetings listed above in that the purpose is to hear from citizens and residents, not to act. Public hearings are subject to the requirements of your state and any additional regulations passed by your council.

Quasi-judicial hearings

This type of meeting is outside the scope of our book. We will mention only that it is critical for elected officials who take part in such hearings to know the rules about ex parte contact (speaking with individuals concerned about the matter outside of the meeting).

Adjourned meetings

An adjourned meeting is the continuation of a meeting that was started earlier.

One of the most unfortunate words in the entire system of Robert's Rules is the word "adjourn." In common usage, the word "adjourn" means to end a meeting, and that is one meaning under Robert's Rules. However, a group can also "adjourn a meeting to a future time"—in other words, continue it. If members gather and there is no quorum (not enough people are present to take action), those who are present can move to "adjourn the meeting" to the next day or another time when, presumably, they will have contacted the absent and recruited enough of them to make the meeting viable. When the "adjourned meeting" resumes, the minutes of the previous meeting up to the point of adjournment are read aloud, in order to bring everyone into the picture.

Open meetings and serial meetings

It is surprising how many ways cities can go wrong with regard to open meetings. Often when a meeting is challenged, the city loses the case. Study the open public meeting requirements of your state carefully. It is far better to be prepared by rigorous attention to the requirements that apply to your jurisdiction.

The courts have found that if several members of a group speak or communicate among each other about a given topic, and then individuals speak with other members, the result may be an illegal "serial meeting." In effect, the members have conspired to agree on a course of action out of the public eye.

It is usually admissible, however, for individual members to speak to each other, or to staff, so long as there is not a "feedback loop" which has the result of a decision being made. If a member of the public seeks to poll all the members of a body, that also is usually acceptable, as long as no one is working to come to a particular conclusion or action.

Alternative meeting formats

Meetings may also be held using nontraditional formats. This table lists some of these methods.

Type	Comments
Meetings by teleconference	If state regulations and your rules of procedure allow, meetings may be held by teleconference. The key from a parliamentary perspective is that during the meeting, each member must be able to hear every other person and be heard, since exchange of views is critical to the process of deliberation.
Unanimous written consent in lieu of a meeting	If law or regulations allow, it is sometimes possible for a council to take action by "unanimous written consent in lieu of a meeting." All members of a body must sign their agreement to the action being proposed, and this written record must be kept with the minutes of the body. Note that if a single person happens to be unavailable (in the hospital, or climbing Mount Kilimanjaro), the action is not valid—every member must sign.
Meetings by email	For most councils and public bodies, meeting by email is not allowed because of the open public meeting requirements. Council members need to know that if they exchange messages among themselves and use the "reply all" function, when more than a quorum is included, the exchange may constitute an illegal secret meeting.
Electronic meetings	This is a whole new arena of parliamentary procedure. The current edition of Robert's Rules has some guidelines on this topic which will be useful for private bodies but are not yet relevant, in our experience, for public ones.

Agendas

The key point to remember about agendas is that they belong to the council. While it is customary and appropriate for the mayor or council president to prepare an agenda for consideration by the body, as presented it is only a draft. The body may make any changes or adjustments it chooses—subject of course to any notice provisions that may apply. For example, if the state has an open meetings law that requires that advance notice of any subject to be taken up be provided, the council cannot then add a new subject on the spot.

It takes a majority vote to change a proposed (draft) agenda. Once an agenda has been adopted, a two-thirds vote is required to change it.

Many councils find a "consent agenda" or "consent calendar" useful. This term refers to a group or "block" of items that are expected to be non-controversial. The method is to adopt this whole batch of items with one single vote—the technical term is "en bloc." Ordinarily, if a member wants to discuss any item on the consent agenda, it is immediately removed and placed on the regular agenda. It could be taken up immediately after the consent agenda, or it could be taken up later in the meeting, wherever it naturally falls.

Some councils require a majority vote before an item can be removed from the consent agenda. We oppose this requirement. Since the purpose is to process a large number of items that are noncontroversial smoothly and quickly, requiring a vote seems to go against the entire idea.

IN OUR EXPERIENCE

I was startled to find a rule in one city's guidelines that an item would be removed from the consent agenda on the demand of any citizen in attendance. To me, this is the road to madness. Let the council determine which subjects it wishes to discuss—it has the authority to do so, which should be left in its hands. —Ann

Sample Agenda

City Council Agenda
City Council Chambers
989 Port Street, First Floor, Dinopolis
January 28, 2013
5:00 p.m.

1. Opening ceremonies – est. 5 minutes
   a. Call to order
   b. Roll call and determination of a quorum
   c. Flag salute
   d. Acceptance of agenda

2. Consent agenda – est. 2 minutes
   Approval of the minutes of the City Council study sessions and
   regular meetings of December 7 and 14, 2012, and special meetings
   of December 15 and 16, 2012.

3. Public comment – est. 20 minutes

4. Regular agenda – est. 60 minutes
   a. A motion to authorize the City's full and final settlement of all claims
      against the City by Peter Pterodactyl upon payment by the City in the
      amount of 200 bales of ginkgo fodder.
   b. Electing Council member Sophia Stegosaurus to the office of Deputy
      Mayor to serve a one-year term through December 31, 2013.
   c. Resolution establishing nondiscrimination policy for City of Dinopolis
      in all public facilities.

5. Report by the City Manager – est. 20 minutes

6. Comments by Council members – est. 15 minutes

7. Adjournment

Minutes

The purpose of minutes is to preserve an accurate record of a council's actions. Council minutes are not intended to inform absent members of all that went on at the meeting they missed, to create a record of the reasons for a council's decision, nor to demonstrate the eloquence and brilliance of elected officials to their public.

Councils should use "action minutes," in which actions are noted briefly and simply. Minutes of this type will include the following items:

- Place of the meeting;
- Time the meeting started and ended;
- Which members of the council were present and, if relevant, any absences;
- The fact that a quorum was present;
- Text of all main motions taken up by the council and their disposition (passed, failed, referred to a committee, postponed etc.);
- If amendments were made, the final version of the motion as amended;
- Any points of order that were made and their resolution; and
- If the council went into executive (secret) session, the time of entering and the time of leaving such session.

If public comment is made, it is ordinarily sufficient to note the fact. Some councils include the names and addresses of those who spoke and some go even further, summarizing the remarks that members of the public make. (At a public hearing, which is a different type of meeting, including the content of remarks is appropriate.)

If council members wish to have more detail in their minutes, another option is "summary minutes." These minutes include a brief listing of the chief arguments that are made for and against different motions, without attribution to any individual. The clerk or secretary must have the capacity to extract those key points from what is said, which can be a challenging task.

The least desirable option is "detailed minutes." This type of minutes is sometimes called "verbatim minutes," which really should apply only to minutes taken by a court recorder who captures every word. In this type of minutes, individual remarks are included along with the name of the person who made them. Detailed minutes are undesirable for several reasons:

- If legal questions arise, delving into the remarks that were made can complicate the council's defense of its actions.
- Clerks must spend substantial time on recording such minutes, which represents an expense that many jurisdictions can ill afford.
- Reviewing, amending and approving detailed minutes can take up great swaths of the council's time; time that would be better spent on more productive activity.
- In searching earlier records, it is hard to extract the key items from among the acres of verbiage included in detailed minutes.

The prevalence of audio and video recording today makes it even more wasteful for councils to invest time and energy in preparing detailed written records of "who said what to whom." Sometimes it seems that the main purpose of such records is to gratify the egos of the speakers. (Note that audio and video recording cannot substitute for written minutes.)

Minutes as prepared by the clerk should be clearly identified as "DRAFT" in the text and the file name. Once they are approved by the body, a clean copy can be prepared that omits the word "draft" and includes the date of approval and appropriate signatures.

Important points about minutes
Minutes are not approved at a special meeting, but are held over until the next regular meeting.
Minutes should not include the name of the seconder of the motion (unless law or regulation requires it).
Minutes should not include routine procedural motions, such as approving the agenda or moving to recess.
Minutes of executive (secret) session, if kept at all, are approved in executive session and filed separately from regular minutes.
A motion that has been withdrawn is not ordinarily included in the minutes.
It is no longer considered appropriate to include the words "respectfully submitted" above the clerk or secretary's signature.

IN OUR EXPERIENCE

One poor clerk told me that after she had prepared detailed minutes of a certain meeting, a council member went up to her and said, "You didn't write down what I meant!" Clerks, like the rest of us, have yet to develop mind-reading abilities.   —Ann

Amendments

A clerk or secretary will need to keep careful track of amendments—who made them, how they are voted on and so on—as they are being discussed. The presider and the members expect this of the clerk and will turn to her for help during the meeting when they are confused themselves.

However, when it comes time to prepare the official minutes, Robert's Rules states that the clerk does not include the details of those amendments, who moved them and how they were voted on. Instead, the minutes should include the final text of the motion as amended. In addition to being sensible and clear, this approach saves the clerk a lot of unnecessary effort.

SAMPLE MINUTES

Meeting Minutes
City Council Regular Meeting
City Council Chambers, 989 Port Street, First Floor, Dinopolis
January 28, 2013
5:00 p.m.

1. The regular meeting of the Dinopolis City Council was called to order in the council chambers on Monday, January 28, at 5:05 p.m., Mayor Pat Pliosaur presiding. Council members Benjamin Brontosaurus, Jasmine Dimetrodon, Sophia Stegorosaurus and Tomas Tyrannosaurus were present. Council member Polly Pteranodon was absent. The meeting was quorate.

2. The consent agenda was approved as presented:
   Minutes of City Council study sessions and regular meetings of December 7 and 14, 2012, and special meetings of December 15 and 16, 2012, approved as presented.

3. Citizens spoke to the Council during the public comment period expressing their gratification at the decrease in taxes and the increase in public services provided during 2012.

4. Regular agenda:
   a. A motion to authorize the City's full and final settlement of all claims against the City by Peter Pterodactyl upon payment by the City in the amount of 200 bales of ginkgo fodder was approved by vote of three in favor, one against. Motion 2013-01.
   b. Council member Sophia Stegosaurus was elected to the office of Deputy Mayor to serve a one-year term through December 13, 2013, by unanimous vote. Motion 2013-02.
   c. A policy establishing a nondiscrimination policy in all public facilities of the City of Dinopolis was passed by unanimous vote: The City of Dinopolis welcomes dinosaurs of all species to its public facilities and does not discriminate on basis of size, number of claws or dietary preference. Motion 2013-03.

5. The City Manager reported on the state of the port's facilities.

6. Council members described recent visits to the public swimming pool, the public hospital and the dinosaur race track.

7. The meeting adjourned at 7:00 p.m.

[signed]
Anthony Ankylosaurus
City Clerk
City of Dinopolis

List of motions

It will also be helpful for the clerk or secretary to maintain a running list of motions passed. Having motions gathered into a single document makes research and verification of actions taken easier.

SAMPLE LIST OF MOTIONS

NUMBER	MOTION	DATE
2013-01	Full and final settlement of all claims against the City by Peter Pterodactyl upon payment by the City in the amount of 200 bales of ginkgo fodder is approved.	1/28/2013
2013-02	Council member Sophia Stegosaurus is elected to the office of Deputy Mayor to serve a one-year term through December 13, 2013.	1/28/2013
2013-03	Policy: The City of Dinopolis welcomes dinosaurs of all species to its public facilities and does not discriminate on basis of size, number of claws or dietary preference.	1/28/2013

Voting

Beyond the principle of one-person, one-vote, the rules of voting can be confusing: Who votes? When do we vote? What's the difference between plurality and majority? What other issues arise when voting?

Who is entitled to vote?

This is an important question from a psychological as well as a legal perspective. For example, many professional organizations distinguish between voting and non-voting members. Only members of the convening body may vote. Guests, staff and onlookers do not vote, nor do they have any rights during a meeting of a council except those established in state law or granted by the council.

Majority vote

A majority vote means more than half (50%) of the votes cast must be in favor to win.

100 people voting	51 in favor
50 people voting	26 in favor
10 people voting	6 in favor
5 people voting	3 in favor

Two-thirds vote

A two-thirds vote means at least two-thirds of the votes cast must be in favor to win. (Two-thirds votes are usually required when the rights of members are to be expanded or limited. For instance, it takes two-thirds voting in favor to cut off debate by means of calling the question.)

100 people voting	67 in favor
50 people voting	34 in favor
10 people voting	7 in favor
5 people voting	4 in favor

Many forms of government have been tried and will be tried in this world of sin and woe. No one pretends that democracy is perfect or all-wise. Indeed, it has been said that democracy is the worst form of government except for all those other forms that have been tried from time to time.

Winston Churchill

Plurality vote

A plurality vote means that the person or proposal receiving the most votes wins.

Total Votes Cast 135	Votes Received	Percentage Received
Sam Stegosaurus	30	22%
Donna Dimetrodon	45	33%
Peter Pterodactyl	20	15%
Theodore T. Rex	40	30%

The winner is Donna Dimetrodon even though she has not received a majority of the votes cast.

Taking the vote

The members must hear the text of the motion again before they vote on it. Normally the presider repeats the motion, but it is fine to have the clerk or secretary read it.

The text of the motion as stated by the presider at this time is the official text which goes in the minutes. If it varies in some significant way from the motion as originally stated (other than because amendments have been adopted), someone should point out the issue. The discrepancy should be resolved before the vote is taken.

The language of voting

Jurassic Parliament recommends that presiders use the question, "Are you ready to vote?" before taking the vote. This is different from the traditional language, which has the presider asking, "Are you ready for the question?" in several instances: *before debate begins, as an invitation to further discussion* and *before the vote is taken.* Using the same verbiage in different situations is confusing. In addition, many people today do not realize that the word "question" in the phrase, "Are you ready for the question?" actually means "the motion we have been discussing."

Here are customary methods of voting and the language the presider should use:

Method	Language to use
Voice or "viva voce"	All those in favor say "aye" [pause]. All those opposed say "no" [pause].
Show of hands	All those in favor raise your right hand and keep it up [pause]. Thank you, hands down. All those opposed raise your right hand and keep it up [pause]. Thank you, hands down.
Counted vote	(Same as above, using the pause to count.)
Voting cards	All those in favor raise your voting card [pause]. Thank you, cards down. All those opposed raise your voting cards [pause]. Thank you, cards down.
Rising or standing vote	All those in favor please rise [pause]. Thank you, be seated. All those opposed please rise [pause]. Thank you, be seated.
Roll call	The clerk will call each member's name. Members will kindly answer "aye" or "no."
Ballot	(Ballots will not ordinarily be acceptable in a local government setting because of the requirements for open public meetings.)

The correct way to ask for a voice vote is to call for "ayes" and "noes." Do not use the word "nays" since it sounds too much like "aye." Even worse, don't say, "All those opposed, same sign." This out-of-date formulation still occurs, but it is very confusing and should not be used.

After calling for those in favor, the presider must call for the negative vote. Even if it seems to the presider that everyone votes in favor, she must still call for the negative, or the vote is not legitimate. This is an ancient principle of parliamentary law and was established to prevent obvious abuses. It applies even on very small bodies such as three-person county commissions.

A two-thirds vote should always be taken by a method that allows the presider to see the result, not by voice.

After taking the vote, the presider announces the result:

"The ayes have it, and the motion passes"
or "The noes have it, and the motion fails."

The presider has a duty to call the results of the vote fairly, and to dispel any doubt or confusion that members may have about the results of the vote. She should be ready to take the vote again if necessary, by using a different method.

Any member who doubts the result of a voice vote may call out the word, "Division!" The presider must then take the vote by a show of hands or a rising vote, so that everyone can ascertain what the outcome is.

If a member wants a counted vote, he must make a motion to that effect, which takes a majority in favor to pass. Presiders should be ready to agree to a counted vote if there seems to be doubt about the results, since the presider is the servant of the group as a whole. If a counted vote is taken, the number voting for and against should be included in the minutes.

In a roll call vote, each member's name and vote is recorded in the minutes.

If a council member opposes an action that is taken by the body, he may request that his vote against the motion, or even his abstention from voting, be included in the minutes. This can protect him from future liability regarding the given action.

A member has the right to change his vote up until the result is announced. After that time, he can change it only with the unanimous consent of the body. Deciding whether to grant this privilege cannot be debated.

Majority of entire membership

One concept that sometimes causes confusion is the requirement that "a majority of the entire membership" vote in favor for a motion to pass.

In a large body, it is usually difficult to obtain the vote of a majority of the entire membership. On a council, however, it can be quite easy. In fact, it may be easier to obtain a vote of the "majority of the entire membership" than to obtain a two-thirds vote. This becomes important with votes like "amend something previously adopted" or "rescind," which have more stringent voting requirements than ordinary motions.

Ties and abstentions

If there are equal numbers of votes in favor and against, the motion does not pass. A tied vote fails. If an election is being conducted, this means that there is "no election" and voting must be repeated until a winner emerges.

Under Robert's Rules of Order, to abstain is to do nothing, and abstentions are not counted. At a meeting, all a person has to do in order to abstain is to remain silent, or not cast a vote.

In large groups, the presider does not vote. In small groups like councils (up to about 12 people), under Robert's Rules the presider has the right to vote. Individual jurisdictions will be subject to differing requirements, and obviously each council must know and abide by the law and regulations affecting it.

Robert says that when there is a tie, even in a large meeting, the presider may vote to break it. It is a less well-known fact that if the vote is close, with only one more positive than negative vote, the presider may vote to create a tie, thereby causing the motion to fail. In either case the presider has discretion as to whether he chooses to vote, or lets the result stand. Another way to phrase this is to say that the presider may vote "when his vote would affect the outcome."

Unanimous consent is a chair's best friend

Unanimous consent is a handy tool that can effectively move a meeting along. It is commonly used for correction and approval of minutes, and is often used to grant requests. A presider who has mastered this method of voting will markedly increase the efficiency of his meetings.

ACCORDING TO ROBERT

...the method of unanimous consent can be used either to adopt a motion without the steps of stating the question and putting the motion to a formal vote, or it can be used to take action without even the formality of a motion. p.54

In cases where there seems to be no opposition in routine business or on questions of little importance, time can often be saved by the procedure of unanimous consent, or as it was formerly also called, general consent. p.54

In effect, unanimous consent is a "fast track" way of voting. It jumps over some of the normal process because no obstacle is expected. If a member doesn't want to take the fast track, all she has to do is to say the single word, "objection." This ends the fast track method and returns everyone to the normal way of processing the given action.

In order to use this method, the presider makes a proposal, and then asks, "Is there any objection?" He then pauses—a good, long, patient pause—to give members time to speak up if they do object. At the end of the pause, he says, "Hearing none, the motion is approved," or whatever the given action was.

When a member says "objection," she doesn't need to say anything more to explain her reasons. The single word tells the group that it will vote in the customary way.

Once this type of vote is taken, members are sometimes surprised to learn that they have voted in favor of a course of action, just by remaining silent. The presider must be careful to educate members, so that they understand how the method works.

The following system was authored by Daniel E. Seabold, PRP, who graciously gave us permission to reprint it here.

How it works: four steps

1. The chair asks whether there is any objection to the proposed action.
2. The chair pauses.

If there is no objection...

3. The chair announces the fact that there has been no objection and...
4. ...states that the action will be taken.

EXAMPLE

Suppose that after debate on a pending motion has begun, the maker of the motion requests permission to withdraw it.

1. The chair asks: "Is there any objection to allowing the member to withdraw the motion?"
2. The chair pauses.
3. If there is no objection, the chair states: "Since there is no objection...
4. ...the motion is withdrawn."

Avoid two common mistakes:

- Provide members with a clear opportunity to object.
- If there is no objection, make it clear that a decision has been reached and what action will be taken.

Quorum

A quorum is the minimum number of members eligible to vote who must be present for business to be done. The quorum may be expressed as a number or as a percentage. If a meeting is started with a quorum and enough members leave during the meeting so that there is not a quorum remaining, the business of the meeting may not continue. If state law does not specify the quorum, the quorum will be a majority of the voting members. Vacancies (if someone has resigned or absconded to the Cayman Islands, for example) are not counted in determining the basis for the quorum unless the council standing rules specify so.

Example of a quorum that is a percentage of the total membership:

> The Dinoville Service Club has a quorum of 10% of its members. Since there are 1000 voting members, 100 members are sufficient to conduct business. The annual meeting regularly draws hundreds of members, so there is no problem.

Example of a quorum that is a majority of the total membership:

> The Dinoville Council of Delegates has 100 members, and the quorum is a majority. It's often difficult to get 51 members to attend the Council meetings which are held every week on Saturday at 6:00 a.m.

When voting and quorum are linked

Usually the quorum requirement is separate from voting requirements. Establishing a quorum simply means that business can take place and voting may be done. The requirements for motions to pass are separate, as outlined above. Sometimes, however, state law or council rules link the two, for example, "A majority of votes cast by the members present and voting are required for a motion to pass, provided that the votes in favor are at least equal to a quorum."

For example, if a council has 9 members and 5 are present at a meeting, a quorum is established and the meeting will proceed. In this case and in common circumstances, only 3 members would make up a majority at a meeting and be able to pass a motion. However, if voting and quorum are linked as in the language above, it would take all 5 present voting in favor to pass a motion.

Part II
Making Sense of Motions

Part II: Making Sense of Motions

Making motions is essential to the system laid out in Robert's Rules of Order. While the specifications are highly detailed, anyone can learn to use motions effectively. Each type of motion serves a specific procedural purpose and has a specific set of characteristics.

In Part II, we provide you with an introduction to the most common and important motions. Examples are provided by the members of the Dinopolis City Council, here to model the correct verbiage when making motions: Jasmine, Benjamin, Sophia, Tomas and Mayor Pat.

Precedence of Motions

IN OUR EXPERIENCE

Properly conducting a meeting is like making a good pot of soup. When all the ingredients are added in the right proportion and in the right order, the soup will be excellent every time. Robert's Rules of Order gives us the recipe. We need only follow it to ensure an excellent (fair and effective) meeting. —Andrew

The matter of "precedence of motions" is sometimes mystifying to the newcomer, but in essence it is rather simple. The principle is that each motion has a number or rank. When motions are pending, motions with a higher rank may be made, but motions with a lower rank are out of order (not allowed). The main motion has the lowest rank, it can be made only if there is no other motion pending.

So, for example, if we are discussing a motion to approve an Arts Festival next summer, and someone has moved to postpone consideration to the next meeting in order to allow staff to provide more information, a motion to amend the motion to hold the festival the year after would be out of order. "Postpone" has the rank of 5, and "amend" has the rank of 3. The amendment will have to wait until we get our hands back on the motion at the next meeting.

There are 13 motions with ranks (see Appendix B. Motions Chart). "Point of order" and "request for information" do not have a rank; they are dealt with immediately. Contrariwise, the "bring back" motions ("amend something previously adopted," "rescind" and "reconsider") have no rank and can only be made if there is no other business on the table, no motion under consideration.

An elected official who takes the time to learn about these ranks, and to apply them, will be far more successful in dealing with council matters than one who yields to internal bafflement and avoids dealing with the entire subject.

Note that the presentation here follows the order which we have found most useful for learning about motions, not the exact ranking of the "precedence of motions."

Whoever strenuously endeavors, him we can rescue.

Goethe

Main Motion (rank 1)

Jasmine: *I move that we build a mammalian outreach center.*

A motion is a proposal to do something. A main motion suggests that a group take some action. It is the first step in the process by which a board or other body takes action. In meetings run according to strict parliamentary procedure, a main motion is necessary before discussion can begin.

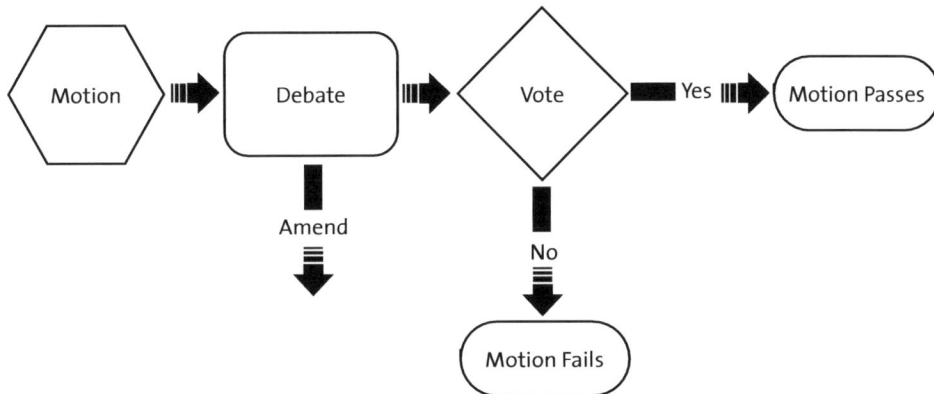

Figure 5. Main Motion

Main motions can only be made when no other motions are pending. In large groups, when the full force of Robert's Rules is in play, the main motion serves to open discussion. When using Robert's small board rules, a main motion can move a group from discussion into action.

Ideas for action take on "standing" when someone is recognized (given permission to speak) by the presider, and uses the words, "I move that..." followed by the proposal.

Any member has an equal right to make motions, though in large meetings, the presider does not do so. The person who makes the motion is called "the mover" or "the maker" of the motion.

Main motions have the following characteristics:
- Should be in writing unless very short.
- Should be clear and unambiguous.
- Should be phrased in the grammatical positive.
- Must comply with the rules of procedure.
- Are in order when no other business is pending.

When someone proposes a course of action, it is a mistake to allow members to say "so moved." Insist that the person making the proposal write it down. This will force the mover of the motion to clarify and refine her own thinking, and also will ensure that everyone is "on the same page" as discussion begins. Though it takes a few minutes, the time spent will pay dividends as discussion continues.

A main motion:
- needs a second,
- can be debated,
- can be amended, and
- takes a majority vote (more than half) to pass.

There are eight steps to process a main motion:

1.	A member makes a motion.
2.	Another member seconds the motion.
3.	The presider states the motion.
4.	Members debate the motion and amend it if they wish to.
5.	When discussion is concluded, the presider restates the motion and calls for the vote.
6.	Members vote.
7.	The presider states the result of the vote, whether the motion passes or fails, and what will happen as a result.
8.	The presider states the next item of business.

Note that once the motion has been made, seconded and stated by the presider, it belongs to the group. It is no longer the "property" of the maker or the seconder. The way that the presider states the motion is its official text, so if a presider changes the words or intent of the maker, the maker should quickly speak up to get the matter put right. Similarly the way that the presider states the motion before the vote is the official text of the motion.

Important points about seconding a motion
Members second a motion because they would like to debate it.
Members may second a motion they disagree with if they would like to discuss it.
It is not necessary to be recognized (given permission to speak) by the presider in order to second a motion. Members may just call out "second."
If no one says "second," the presider may ask, "Is there a second?"
If no one then speaks up, the presider should say, "The motion will not be taken up for lack of a second" and move immediately to the next item of business.
Do not second motions just to be polite!

EXAMPLE

Jasmine: *I move that we build a mammalian outreach center.*
Benjamin [without being recognized]: *Second!*
Mayor Pat: *It has been moved and seconded that we build a mammalian outreach center. We will now debate the motion.*

[Members debate the motion]

Mayor Pat: *Are you ready to vote? The motion is that we build a mammalian outreach center.*
All those in favor say "aye." [Members in favor speak up.]
All those opposed say "no." [Members opposed speak up.]
The "ayes" have it, the motion passes, and we will build a mammalian outreach center. The Building Committee will take the next steps. Our next item of business is...

Amendment (rank 3a)

Tomas: *I move that we amend the motion by adding the words "in the Okaachooku Swamp."*

To amend a motion means to change a motion or improve it because you've come up with a better idea.

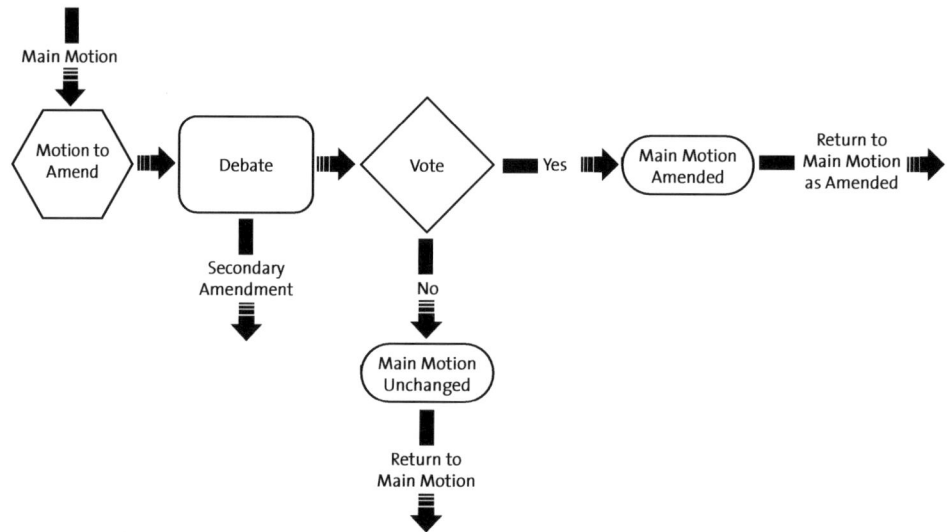

Figure 6. Amendment

Amendments must be germane, which means "related" or "relevant." If there is a question, the presider decides whether an amendment is germane or not. (If there is a challenge to this decision, however, the group has the final say.)

Amendment:
- needs a second,
- can be debated,
- can be amended, and
- takes a majority vote to pass.

Motions may be amended in several different ways:
- Add or insert words.
- Strike out words.
- Strike out and add or insert words.
- Substitute.

To add words is to place them at the end of the text of the motion; to insert words is to place them within the motion.

Important points about amendments
Amendments are discussed and voted on before the main motion in order to make the main motion as good as it can be (to "perfect" the motion).
Once a motion has been amended, it can be amended again if the proposed amendment applies to another aspect of the motion.
The only limit to the number of amendments is the patience of your group.
Amendments may be made at any time during debate.
It takes special actions to go back and change something already amended.
Amendments cannot negate the original motion, or convert one parliamentary motion into another.
Amendment by substituting has several tricky aspects.

EXAMPLE

Jasmine: *I move that we build a mammalian outreach center.*
Benjamin [without being recognized]: *Second!*
Mayor Pat: *It has been moved and seconded that we build a mammalian outreach center. We will now debate the motion.*

[Members debate the motion. During the debate...]

Sophia: *I move that we amend the motion by adding the words "in the Okaachooku Swamp."*
Tomas [without being recognized]: *Second!*
Mayor Pat: *It has been moved and seconded that we amend the motion by adding the words "in the Okaachooku Swamp." We will now debate the motion to amend.*

[Members debate the motion.]

Mayor Pat: *Are you ready to vote on the amendment? The motion is that we add the words "in the Okaachooku Swamp" to the motion. If passed, the motion will read, "that we build a mammalian center in the Okaachooku Swamp."*
All those in favor say "aye." [Members in favor speak up.]
All those opposed say "no." [Members opposed speak up.]
The "ayes" have it, the motion passes, and our main motion now reads "that we build a mammalian center in the Okaachooku Swamp." We will now continue debate on the motion as amended.

[Members continue debate.]

Mayor Pat: *Are you ready to vote? The motion is that we build a mammalian outreach center in the Okaachooku Swamp.*
All those in favor say "aye." [Members in favor speak up.]
All those opposed say "no." [Members opposed speak up.]
The "ayes" have it, the motion passes, and we will build a mammalian outreach center in the Okaachooku Swamp. The Building Committee will take the next steps. Our next item of business is...

What is a friendly amendment?

ACCORDING TO ROBERT

The term "friendly amendment" is often used to describe an amendment offered by someone who is in sympathy with purposes of the main motion, in the belief that the amendment will either improve the statement or effect of the main motion, presumably to the satisfaction of its maker, or will increase the chances of the main motion's adoption. Regardless of whether or not the maker of the main motion "accepts" the amendment, it must be opened to debate and voted on formally (unless adopted by unanimous consent) and is handled under the same rules as amendments generally. p.162

An amendment is a proposal to change a motion (a proposed action) being considered by a group. Sometimes people suggest amendments with the intention of making the original motion ineffective, or defeating its purpose. These are hostile amendments, offered with negative intent.

Sometimes people suggest amendments that they sincerely believe will improve the original motion. These are friendly amendments, offered with positive intent.

An unfortunate custom has arisen whereby when a person suggests a "friendly amendment," the presider often turns to the maker of the motion to ask him if he would accept the amendment. If he agrees, the presider sometimes also asks the seconder if she would accept the amendment.

This is wrong!

Once a motion has been made, seconded and stated by the chair, it belongs to the group as a whole, not to the individual who first proposed it. It is the group as a whole that must accept or reject any proposed amendment, whatever the intent of the proposer. The maker of the motion, and the seconder, have the same rights as the other members of the group—no more and no less.

When someone offers a friendly amendment, we suggest that the presider say, "A friendly amendment is handled just like any other amendment. Is there a second?" This language does not make people feel stupid, but sets the group on the right procedural path.

If the presider turns to the original maker of the motion to ask if he approves of the proposed change, any member can say, "point of order." This stops the action. The member can then explain the error. (See page 59 for more on "point of order.")

Secondary amendment (rank 3b)

Jasmine: *I move that we amend the motion to amend by adding the words "on the north shore."*

When a group amends a main motion, the motion they use is called "primary amendment." It is also possible to amend an amendment while it is being considered. This is called a "secondary amendment." The "secondary amendment" applies only to the "primary amendment."

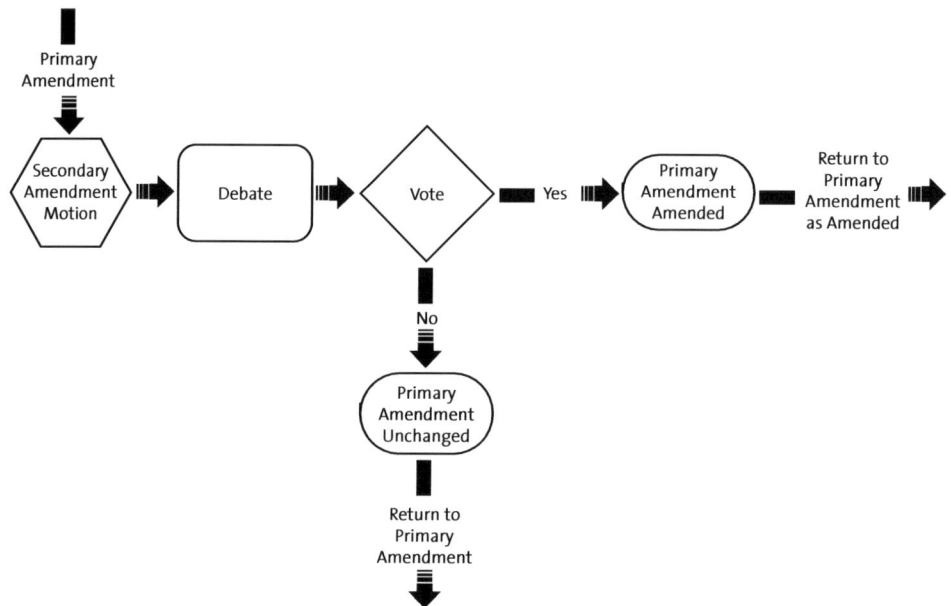

Figure 7. Secondary Amendment

A secondary amendment:
- requires a second,
- can be debated, and
- takes a majority vote to pass,
- but it cannot be amended; this is the case, logically enough, because the process has to end somewhere.

A secondary amendment modifies a primary amendment by the usual methods:
- Add or insert words.
- Strike out words.
- Strike out and add or insert words.
- Substitute.

As with the previous motion, the group votes on this motion before it votes on the amendment that it modifies.

IN OUR EXPERIENCE

People get quite nervous when someone talks about "amending the amendment," but this motion isn't as daunting as it seems. Understanding how to use it can prove very helpful. It's also important to remember that once you've reached a "secondary amendment," you can't keep going. No tertiary amendments are allowed! —Ann

Refer to Committee (rank 4)

Sophia: *I move that we refer this motion to the Building Committee to report back with a recommendation at next month's meeting.*

Motion to refer to committee allows a board or other group to send a proposal off to a smaller group to review, discuss and recommend what to do.

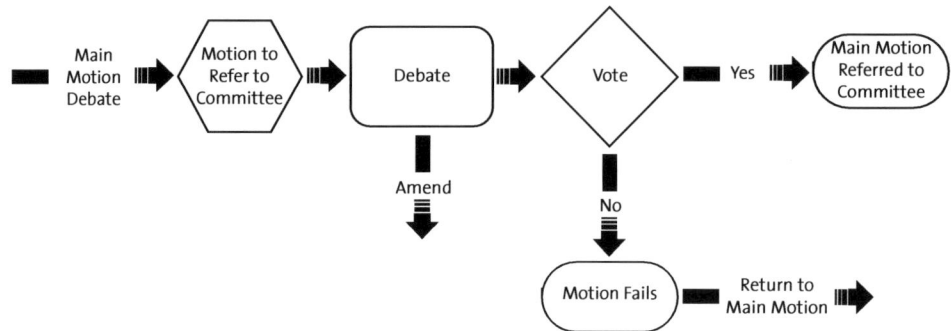

Figure 8. Refer to Committee

In making this motion, the maker must specify three things: which committee the motion is going to, when it is coming back and whether the committee has the power to decide the matter, or is merely making a recommendation. If not otherwise specified, a motion is sent to a committee for a recommendation.

Refer to committee:
- needs a second,
- can be debated,
- can be amended as to which committee the motion is referred to, and when it comes back, and
- takes a majority vote to pass.

EXAMPLE

Jasmine: *I move that we build a mammalian outreach center.*
Benjamin [without being recognized]: *Second!*
Mayor Pat: *It has been moved and seconded that we build a mammalian outreach center. We will now debate the motion.*

[Members debate the motion. During debate...]

Sophia: *I move that we refer this motion to the Building Committee to report back with a recommendation at next month's meeting.*
Tomas [without being recognized]: *Second!*
Mayor Pat: *It has been moved and seconded that we refer this motion to the Building Committee to report back with a recommendation at next month's meeting. We will now debate the motion to refer.*

[Members debate the motion]

Mayor Pat: *Are you ready to vote? The motion is that we refer this motion to the Building Committee to report back with a recommendation at next month's meeting.*
All those in favor say "aye." [Members in favor speak up.]
All those opposed say "no." [Members opposed speak up.]
The "ayes" have it, the motion passes, and the motion is referred to the Building Committee. Our next item of business is...

Postpone to a Definite Time (rank 5)

Sophia: *I move that we postpone consideration of this motion to next month's meeting so we have time to think about it.*

Postpone to a definite or certain time is a very useful motion. When members say, "I would like to table this until our next meeting," they should actually be moving to postpone the motion until the next meeting.

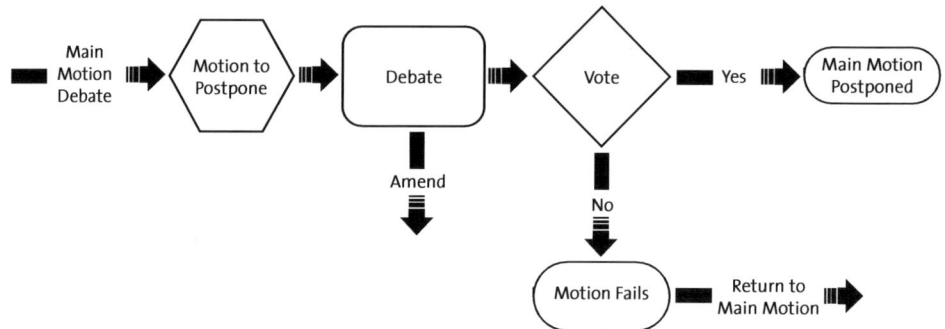

Figure 9. Postpone to a Definite Time

This motion:
- requires a second,
- can be debated as far as its own merits—cannot discuss the motion that might be postponed except as it pertains to the merits of this motion,
- can be amended, and
- takes a majority to pass.

Motions may be postponed only until the next business meeting if it falls within a quarterly (three month) interval. Don't let anybody move to postpone something until the turn of the century or the apocalypse. If a motion requires more time to be studied, most likely "refer to committee" will be the right motion to use.

EXAMPLE

Jasmine: *I move that we build a mammalian outreach center.*

Benjamin [without being recognized]: *Second!*

Mayor Pat: *It has been moved and seconded that we build a mammalian outreach center. We will now debate the motion.*

[Members debate the motion. During debate...]

Sophia: *I move that we postpone consideration of this motion to next month's meeting so we have time to think about it.*

Tomas [without being recognized]: *Second!*

Mayor Pat: *It has been moved and seconded that we postpone consideration of this motion to next month's meeting so we have time to think about it. We will now debate the motion to postpone.*

[Members debate the motion.]

Mayor Pat: *Are you ready to vote? The motion is that we postpone consideration of this motion to next month's meeting so we have time to think about it.*

All those in favor say "aye." [Members in favor speak up.]

All those opposed say "no." [Members opposed speak up.]

The "ayes" have it, the motion passes, and the motion is postponed to next month's meeting. Our next item of business is...

Table (rank 8)

To "table" is not debatable and takes a majority to pass—making it a dangerous motion, because it is relatively easy to pass when members perhaps do not understand the consequences. Many people think that this is the way to get something out of the way, in other words to kill it. Under Robert's Rules, that would be wrong. It is out of order to table a motion in order to kill it.

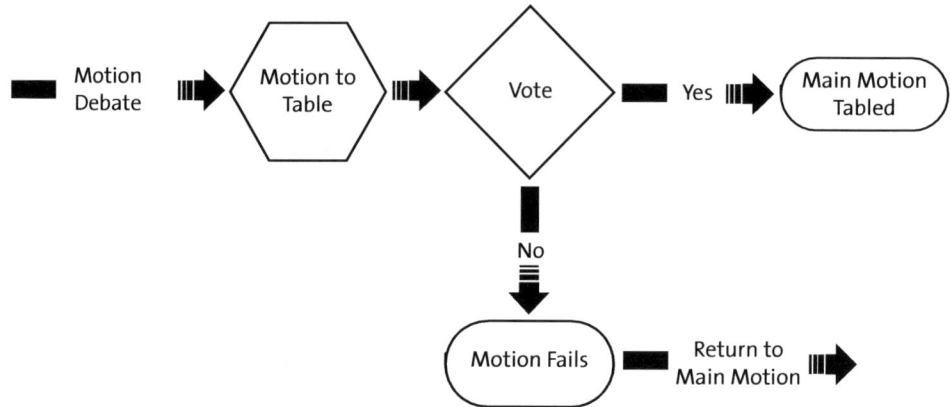

Figure 10. Table

If the presider suspects that the maker wants to kill the motion, she should ask, "For what purpose does the member seek to table the motion?" The legitimate purpose is to put something temporarily aside ("on the table") until the group has dealt with another item. For example, if a speaker has arrived early and the group does not want to continue debate in the presence of an outsider, the pending motion may be "tabled" so that the speaker can give his presentation. Once that item is finished, there must be a motion to "take from the table."

This motion:
- requires a second,
- cannot be debated,
- cannot be amended, and
- takes a majority to pass.

Note that if a motion is not "taken from the table" during the same session or the next regular business session (provided that the next regular business session occurs within a quarterly interval, or the next three months), it dies.

See "postpone indefinitely" on page 68 for a motion that can be helpful to members wishing to kill a motion.

Call the Question (rank 7)

Sophia: *I call the question and move that we stop debate.*

This motion may be the most commonly misunderstood motion. Many people mistakenly believe that if someone shouts out "question," the group must take a vote immediately. This would give a single individual the right to shut down the debate and make everyone vote. Such an outcome would violate the principle that all members have equal rights, privileges and obligations.

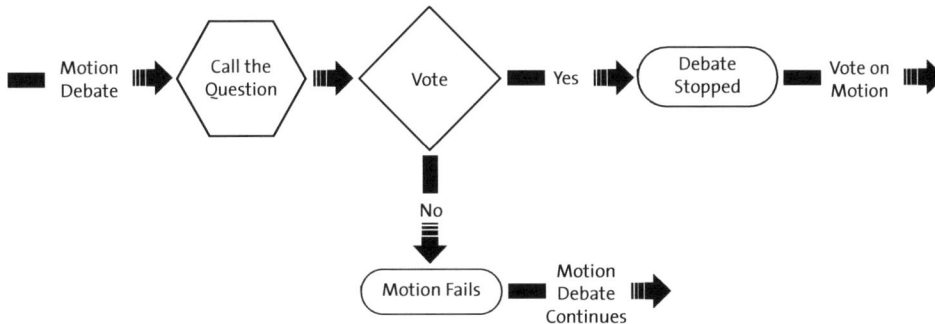

Figure 11. Call the Question

This motion means that one person believes it is time to stop debate and vote immediately on the pending question. It is a request, not an order.

Members must be recognized before calling the question. Don't let someone shout out "question" and take over the meeting without having obtained permission to speak.

When the question is called, the chair asks, "Is there a second?" If someone seconds the motion, the vote is taken immediately on the pending question. It takes two-thirds in favor for this motion to pass.

Call the question:
- needs a second,
- cannot be debated,
- cannot be amended, and
- takes a two-thirds vote to pass. (Under Robert's Rules of Order, a two-thirds vote is normally required when members' rights are being limited or expanded.)

Note that these terms all mean the same thing:
- Call the question
- Previous question
- Move the previous question

EXAMPLE

Jasmine: *I move that we build a mammalian outreach center.*
Benjamin: [without being recognized]: *Second!*
Mayor Pat: *It has been moved and seconded that we build a mammalian outreach center. We will now debate the motion.*

[Members debate the motion. During debate...]

Sophia: *I call the question.*
Tomas [without being recognized]: *Second!*
Mayor Pat: *It has been moved and seconded that we stop debate and vote on the pending question, the motion to build a mammalian outreach center.*
All those in favor of stopping debate and voting now, raise your right hand. [Members raise hands.]
Thank you, hands down.
All those opposed, raise your right hand. [Members raise hands.]
Thank you, hands down.
[If the ayes have it:] *There are two-thirds in favor and we will vote immediately.*
All those in favor of building a mammalian outreach center, say "aye."
[etc.]
[If the noes have it] *There are not two-thirds in favor and debate will continue. Next speaker please...*

IN OUR EXPERIENCE

If you want to alarm people, you can tell them that this is a "vote on whether to vote," which sounds worse than it really is. The term "previous question" is an unhappy leftover from the 19th century. The words meant something completely different in the British parliament. We believe that it would be better to rename this motion as "motion to stop debate" or "motion to vote immediately." —Ann

Point of Order

A point of order is a claim that something procedural is being done wrong. In essence, it is a cry of "mistake." Point of order may interrupt a speaker.

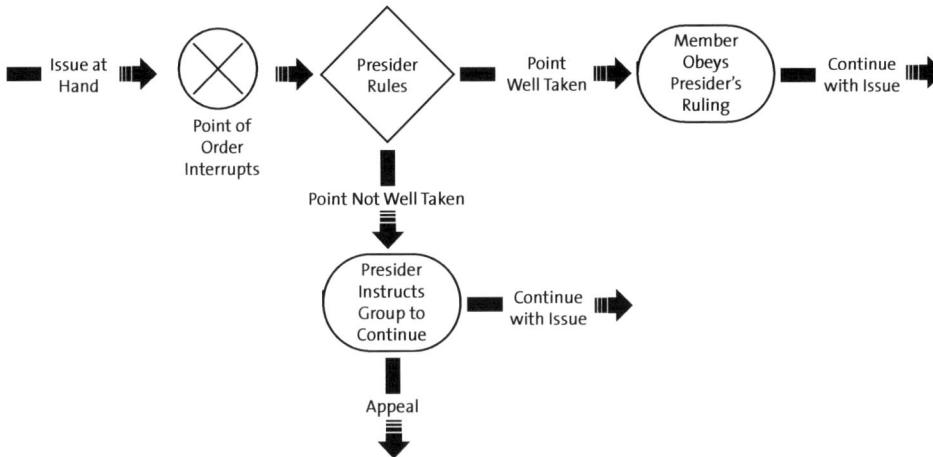

Figure 12. Point of Order

Ordinarily, this motion must be made in a timely manner. The presider rules on the motion. However, any two members can appeal the chair's ruling, and the group is the ultimate authority.

Point of order requires:
- no second,
- no debate,
- no amendment, and
- no vote—the presider rules.

The normal way this happens is that a member of the body makes the claim. He seeks recognition, and may interrupt someone who is speaking to do so. Once he has been given the floor, he says, "I rise to a point of order." The presiding officer replies, "State your point." He then explains the issue. Once the issue is clear, the presiding officer gives a ruling: "The point is well taken," if she agrees, or, "The point is not well taken," if she does not.

Sometimes members say "point of order," because they've heard the term, but aren't quite sure what the motion actually means or can't express clearly the point they are trying to make. If someone says "point of order" but then rambles or seems confused, the presider should ask, "What rule is being broken?"

A point of order must be made in a timely manner. Members must raise the point just as soon as the offense occurs. If they fail to raise it immediately and other business takes place, it is then too late to raise it (with a few exceptions).

If the presider doesn't want to rule on a point of order, it is fine to ask the group to vote on the matter immediately. This can be a good way to turn down the heat.

EXAMPLE

Jasmine: *Madam Mayor, I rise to a point of order.*

Mayor Pat: *State your point.*

Jasmine: *My esteemed colleague from Dinopolis has used the term "cream-faced loon" in referring to the mayor of our fair city. According to Robert's Rules, insults are not allowed in debate.*

Mayor Pat: *The point is well taken. Members will refrain from using improper language.*

IN OUR EXPERIENCE

Robert's Rules of Order Newly Revised *gives members the right to make this motion, but we believe that it is also good for a council when staff are empowered to raise points of order. I once heard a tale of how a new mayor, emerging from executive session called to consider candidates to fill a vacancy on the council, immediately administered the oath of office to the appointee. This is not good! Newly elected officials often need help if they are to fulfill their duties properly. A clerk or other staff person should be empowered, by custom or policy, to say, "Point of order, Mr. Mayor. Under the Open Public Meetings Act, council must vote in public to appoint this candidate before the oath can be administered."* —Ann

In some cities the clerk serves as parliamentarian, so he may be already authorized to speak. If a council does not have this arrangement, authorization can be included in the rules of procedure. There are many benefits to doing this. By virtue of their job and experience, clerks are very familiar with the rules. They can help elected officials act properly and protect the municipality from liability. Making it easy for them to speak up will benefit the city, help create a climate of transparency and openness, and assist the mayor and council members in doing their job.

Appeal

If the members disagree with the presider's ruling on a point of order, or with *any ruling or decision of the presider,* any two members can appeal. In that case, the group itself will decide what is correct.

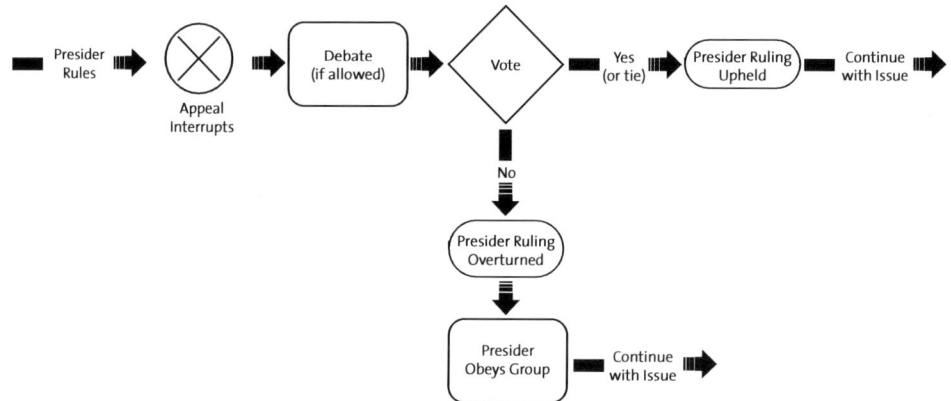

Figure 13. Appeal

Note that appeals must be seconded. Some appeals can be debated, and some cannot. (It seems sensible to us that appeals relating to decorum can't be debated—since people will have different ideas about what is insulting and what is acceptable language, and debating could stretch things out to the millennium.)

It is important for any presider to understand this motion and know how to conduct the vote, since few people have experience of it, and the method can be confusing. The motion being voted on is:

"Shall the presider's decision be upheld?"

This means that if you agree with the presider, you vote in favor. If you disagree, you vote against. It takes a majority vote against to overturn the presider's decision. This is a bit counterintuitive, since the member who appeals takes a stand *against the presider's decision,* but voting yes on the appeal means that you *agree with the presider.* It's critical for a presider who encounters this situation to explain the method very carefully, so everyone knows what is being decided.

These are the steps:

1. Presider speaks first and explains reason for ruling.

2. (If appeal is debatable) Members debate the matter, each member speaking once.

3. Presider speaks again to sum up.

4. Members vote.

5. The appeal is decided by majority vote of the members.
   - If members vote in favor, presider's decision is upheld.
   - If members vote against, presider's decision is not upheld.
   - If there is a tie, then the presider's decision is upheld.

It could be argued that the motion to appeal is the heart of Robert's Rules. Robert's system is deeply and profoundly democratic (no reference to political parties intended). The presider is the servant of the group and the group is the final authority.

EXAMPLE

Tomas: *I appeal the decision of the chair on the grounds that "cream-faced loon" is a literary reference and not an insult.*

Benjamin: *Second!*

Mayor Pat: *Very well, since the ruling of the chair has been appealed, the group will decide. Note that appeals pertaining to proper use of language and decorum may not be debated. All those who believe "cream-faced loon" is an insult, please say "aye." All who believe that it is not an insult, please say "no."*

[If the ayes have it:] *The ayes have it, the ruling of the chair is upheld and members will refrain from using that term.*

[If the noes have it:] *The noes have it, the ruling of the chair is not upheld and members may use the term.*

Request for Information

Jasmine: *I rise to make a request for information, Madam Mayor.*
Mayor Pat: *State your question.*
Jasmine: *Is there any city-owned land in the Okaachooku Swamp?*

Formerly known as "point of information," request for information is a question. It is a request for some information that is relevant to the debate and somewhat urgent.

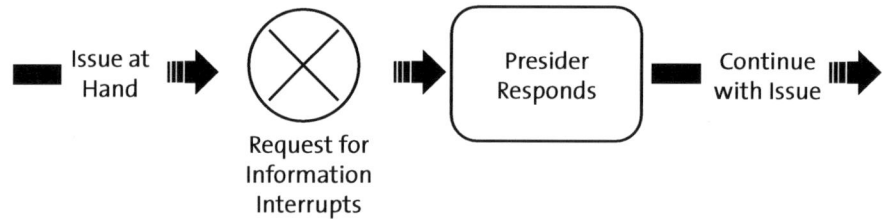

Figure 14. Request for Information

The presider should respond to the motion by saying, "State your question." Once the member has stated his question, there are three ways to answer: the presider may give the answer, the presider may refer the question to someone else who is present or the presider may say, "We will get back to you later."

Request for information requires:
- no second,
- no debate,
- no amendment, and
- no vote—the presider rules.

Sometimes members misunderstand the purpose of this motion. They may rise and say "point of information" or "point of clarification" and then proceed to provide information to their colleagues. This is actually debate—presenting one's opinion—and the presider should not allow it. In such a case, the presider can ask, "What piece of information does the member need in order to decide how to vote?" This will return the focus to the immediate issue.

Raising a request for information does not count as "debate." If a member raises such a motion, he is still entitled to speak on the matter being discussed.

Note that the presider is not obliged to answer hypothetical questions.

Three "Bring-back" Motions

These three motions are examples of a main motion of a special type, an incidental main motion. An incidental main motion relates to the business of the group or its past or future action, but does not mean that the group is taking up a new topic. It may be moved only when no other business is pending.

The bring-back motions present the group with a potential action on a motion that was previously resolved.

Amend something previously adopted

This motion allows the group to change something it did previously.

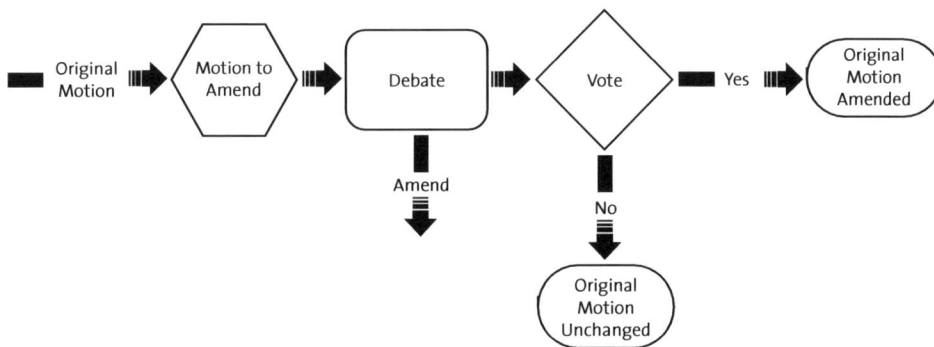

Figure 15. Amend Something Previously Adopted

Amend something previously adopted:
- requires a second,
- can be debated, and
- can be amended.

However, because it should not be done lightly, it requires either a **two-thirds vote** (if taken up at the same meeting) or **previous notice** or a **majority of the entire membership**. Notice may be given orally at a meeting or in writing when the agenda for the next meeting is distributed.

Rescind

Rescinding a motion voids or cancels the motion in question.

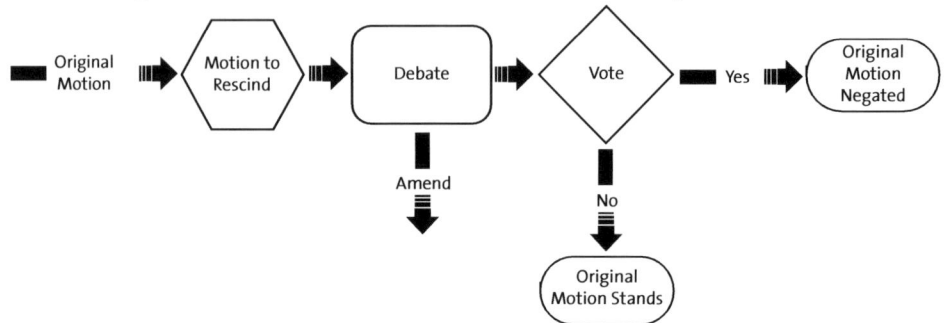

Figure 16. Rescind

Rescind:
- requires a second,
- can be debated, and
- can be amended.

It requires either a **two-thirds vote** (if taken up at the same meeting) or **previous notice or a majority of the entire membership**.

Note that if the motion has already been acted on, it may not be possible to rescind it. Consult a knowledgeable attorney about the proper steps to take back or void an action in this case. Similarly, if the action involved a resignation, an election or an expulsion from office, and the person was present or has been officially notified, it can't be undone.

Reconsider

Confusion sometimes results when members suggest "we should reconsider this" but what they mean is "we should think about it and maybe change our minds." The word "reconsider" has a specific parliamentary meaning and requires certain conditions. When a member asks to "reconsider something," the presider should help the member determine which of the three motions is best: "amend something previously adopted," "rescind" or "reconsider."

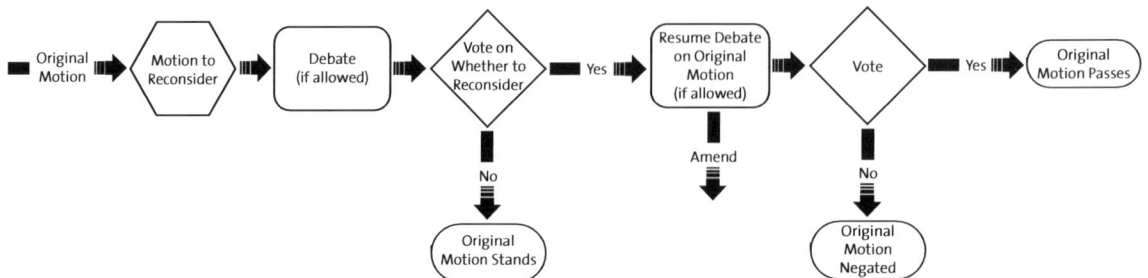

Figure 17. Reconsider

When you "reconsider" something, you take it up again as if it had never been decided. The slate is wiped clean and debate begins where you left off, just before the vote was taken.

Reconsider:
- requires a second,
- can be debated if the original motion was debatable,
- cannot be amended, and
- takes a majority to pass.

Under Robert's Rules this motion has two additional peculiarities:
1. It can be moved only on the same day or the next day.
2. It must be moved by someone who voted with the prevailing side, the majority.

It is important to recognize that this motion, if it passes, will involve two steps:
1. Voting on the question of whether to reconsider.
2. Debating, amending and voting on the motion at issue (if debatable and amendable).

Note that under Robert's Rules, a motion that is defeated may ordinarily be introduced again or "renewed" at a future meeting or session.

In Our Experience

People can get very confused when the word "reconsider" is used. I once had an indirect exchange with the attorney for a utility district who maintained that if the utility commission wanted to reconsider something, it would have required a two-thirds affirmative vote by all the registered voters in the district. This position was nonsensical and missed the basic point that "the body" governing the utility district is its elected commissioners, not the voters. People sometimes think that the person who seconded the motion must have voted with the prevailing side in order to reconsider something. Don't let these peculiar misunderstandings happen to you!   —Ann

Postpone Indefinitely (rank 2)

The simplest way to kill a motion is to vote it down. If, however, the members do not want to be on the record as voting against a motion, they can move to postpone the motion indefinitely. This has a very low rank—only a main motion is lower.

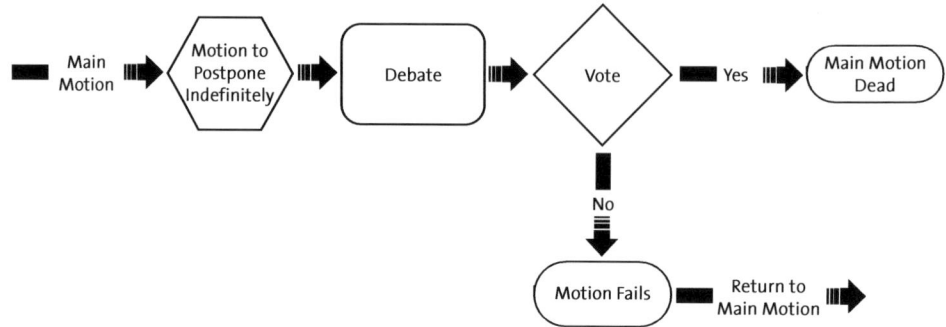

Figure 18. Postpone Indefinitely

Postpone indefinitely:
- needs a second,
- can be debated, and debate may go into the main question,
- cannot be amended, and
- takes a majority to pass.

IN OUR EXPERIENCE

When people move "to table the motion" in an effort to kill it, what they really should use is the motion "to postpone indefinitely." It is proper for the presider to make a suggestion to members so that they can achieve their goals using the right procedure. You may have to put up with a few giggles when people hear the name of this motion, but it is a perfectly correct motion to use. —Ann

Withdrawing a Motion

A motion may be withdrawn by the mover only with the permission of the group. The mover may ask to withdraw a motion and the chair then can ask for objections. If there are none, the motion is withdrawn. If there is an objection, then a vote must be taken and the motion withdrawn only with a majority vote. Ordinarily, withdrawn motions are not included in the minutes.

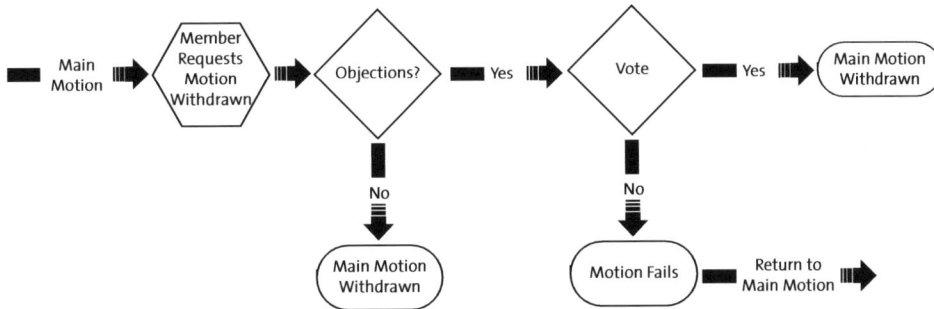

Figure 19. Withdrawing a Motion

IN OUR EXPERIENCE

Under the rules of parliamentary procedure, you don't get to say, "I'm taking my marbles and going home." We have heard of an instance when members of a council were hotly debating a controversial motion. When the maker realized that it was likely to fail, in order to avoid an outright defeat he said "I withdraw the motion." His colleagues allowed him to do this and did not object, which they had the right to do. Their political aims would have been better served if they had known the rules and said, "This motion belongs to the council and we will not allow it to be withdrawn."   —Ann

Part III

Discussion

Part III: Discussion

While free-flowing conversation can, and often does, lead to action, it is rarely efficient. By establishing and adhering to a set of rules and guidelines, a council will best utilize its most important resource—a council member's time. In Part III we:

- Offer the most basic rules for discussion;
- Examine Robert's Rules for small groups;
- Share guidelines for more effective interaction; and
- Provide a system for efficient and fair debate.

Seven Basic Rules

Here is a distillation of the basic rules for discussion under Robert's Rules and common parliamentary law. They are collected from different places within the book. Having a clear understanding of these basics is critical for successful meetings of any type.

All members have an equal right to speak and make motions.

> **ACCORDING TO ROBERT**
> *A member of an assembly, in the parliamentary sense, is a person entitled to full participation in its proceedings, that is, the right to attend meetings, to make motions, to speak in debate, and to vote. p. 3*

This rule, so obvious and innocuous, is sometimes not applied in practice. While every member has equal rights, circumstances sometimes prevent members from exercising them fully. These recommendations, when properly applied, empower all members, and make them far more likely to participate in discussion and debate.

An association of men who will not quarrel with one another is a thing which has never yet existed, from the greatest confederacy of nations down to a town meeting or a vestry.

Thomas Jefferson

Nonmembers do not have the right to speak or to make motions.

According to Robert
Any nonmembers allowed in the hall during a meeting, as guests of the organization, have no rights with reference to the proceedings. p. 648

This means that at your meetings, members of the public, citizens, residents, visiting bigwigs or the King of Spain do not have the right to discuss what you are doing as you do it. A council must distinguish between discussion by and among its members, which is the way it accomplishes its work, and public comment. Members of the public have the right to provide information and input, to make suggestions, to criticize or to praise, but not to take part in the council's discussion, nor to attempt to interject themselves into an ongoing debate.

A council may, by majority vote, give or deny permission for any member of the public to speak during council meetings.

Sometimes, amidst strong emotion or opinions from the public, council meetings go on too long and lose their way. Setting clear rules and sticking to them is essential for every council. It may not seem necessary in sunny days, but when dark storms of controversy arise, the council will be glad for this.

In Our Experience
Confusion about when citizens may speak can lead to very unprofessional and disorderly meetings. See YouTube for disheartening examples of chaos, bad language and meeting breakdown. —Ann

One subject is discussed at a time.

According to Robert
[In the year 1581 the clerk of the British House of Commons wrote this rule:] *When a Motion has been made that Matter must receive a Determination by the Question, or be laid aside by the general Sense of the House, before another be entertain'd. pp. xxxiii-xxxiv*

This is a critical rule for efficiency. Human nature being what it is, and the interconnectedness of life being what it is, people tend to wander off topic or to start topics that are related to, but different from, the topic being discussed. It is crucial for the presider and the members to help everyone keep on track and discuss one subject at a time. Robert's Rules provides very useful scaffolding in which to do this, including ways to defer a subject if another item is more time-sensitive, or to postpone a motion if the group does not have the information it needs to discuss it effectively at that time.

One person speaks at a time.

This is another significant difference between personal conversation and the discussion of a subject by a governing body. People must never talk over one another during a council meeting.

No interrupting.

> **ACCORDING TO ROBERT**
>
> *When a member has been assigned the floor and has begun to speak—unless he begins to discuss a subject when no motion is pending or speaks longer in debate than the rules of the assembly allow—he cannot be interrupted by another member or by the chair except for one of the following purposes, and then only when the urgency of the situation justifies it... pp. 383-384*
>
> *Although the presiding officer should give close attention to each speaker's remarks during debate, he cannot interrupt the person who has the floor so long as that person does not violate any of the assembly's rules and no disorder arises. The presiding officer must never interrupt a speaker simply because he knows more about the matter than the speaker does. pp. 43-44*

It is common practice in conversation for participants to interrupt each other. This is not allowed in any meeting conducted according to Robert's Rules (unless the rules are broken—see "When the Rules Are Broken" on page 95). Let the member who has the floor speak.

The most common form of human stupidity is forgetting what one is trying to do.

Friedrich Nietzsche

Courtesy and respect are required at all times.

> **ACCORDING TO ROBERT**
>
> *Speakers must address their remarks to the chair, maintain a courteous tone, and—especially in reference to any divergence of opinion—should avoid injecting a personal note into debate. p. 43*
>
> *When a question is pending, a member can condemn the nature or likely consequences of the proposed measure in strong terms, but he must avoid personalities, and under no circumstances can he attack or question the motives of another member. p. 392*

This is a bottom-line and elemental rule that must be followed by everyone. Courtesy and respect covers a wide range of actions. It is not in order to engage in personal attacks, to insult people by innuendo, to use insults, epithets or profanity, to roll one's eyes, sigh and shrug, or to boo, hiss or clap. While geography, culture and custom may affect a group's definition of which of these things are offensive, every group should define the behavior it will not tolerate, institute the appropriate rules, and then enforce them.

No one may speak a second time until everyone who wishes to do so has spoken once.

> **ACCORDING TO ROBERT**
>
> *No one is entitled to the floor a second time in debate on the same motion on the same day as long as any other member who has not spoken on this motion desires the floor. p. 31; see also p. 379*

This is perhaps the most neglected rule in all of Robert's Rules of Order. Many people do not even know that this rule exists. When discussing a subject, it is vital that each person who wants to speak can be heard.

This is the arena where "council discussion" differs the most from "conversation." As mentioned above, we're so used to the back-and-forth of everyday conversation that we think of it as the ordinary and usual way to discuss things. For council meetings, however, the conversational style is usually not effective. Extroverts dominate and introverts are left out. The "round robin" method, pp. 88-91, is one way to ensure that this rule is followed.

Small Board Discussion

Robert's Rules of Order provides special rules for small groups. As previously mentioned, it describes a small board as "up to about 12 people." However, in our experience slightly larger bodies, up to about 20 people, may also benefit from small board rules.

Some of these rules are very useful, and some of them are less so. If a council has adopted *Robert's Rules of Order Newly Revised* as its parliamentary authority, and has 12 or fewer members, then the group is already authorized to use these small board rules.

Even in this case, the council should review the issues and adopt the specific rules that suit its needs and culture best. Taking the time to review rules of procedure and consider which work well helps the members internalize these rules, remember them and apply them in the heat of discussion and debate.

In this section are recommendations with the relevant quotes from *Robert's Rules of Order Newly Revised*. Appendix C is a list of the essential rules for discussion and debate, including these small board rules, for reference.

Where wise actions are the fruit of life, wise discourse is the pollination.

Bryant H. McGill

The presider may participate in debate.

> **ACCORDING TO ROBERT**
>
> [In formal debate] *Except in committees and small boards, the presiding officer should not enter into discussion of the merits of pending questions.* p.43
>
> *Normally, especially in a large body, he* [the presider] *should have nothing to say on the merits of pending questions.* p.394
>
> [For small groups] *If the chairman is a member, he may, without leaving the chair, speak in informal discussion and in debate, and vote on all questions.* [Footnote:] *Informal discussion may be initiated by the chairman himself, which in effect, enables the chairman to submit his own proposals without formally making a motion (although he has the right to make a motion if he wishes).* p.488

While these quotes may seem confusing at first glance, they illustrate the distinction that Robert's Rules makes between large bodies and small boards. In formal debate with large groups, the presiding officer focuses almost entirely on process, guiding the members in debate and resolution. For small groups, the presider may participate more fully.

However, while it is true that in small groups the presider may debate and make motions, restraint is advisable. Even in smaller boards, a presider who chooses to be a facilitator will prove most effective.

Therefore, as previously mentioned, we recommend that presiders speak and debate last, after everyone has had a chance. This is a Jurassic Parliament position that differs from Robert's Rules. Besides making the presider more impartial, this also allows her to sum up the debate, which can be critical in helping everyone see the big picture.

Likewise, we maintain that presiders ought not to make motions. It is always better for other members to propose motions, because of the human tendency to show undue deference to the leader of a group.

The rule and custom of the particular council and the applicable state and local laws should determine whether the presider may vote. In small councils it may make sense for the presider to vote.

Informal discussion without a motion is allowed.

> **ACCORDING TO ROBERT**
>
> [In formal debate] *Until a matter has been brought before the assembly in the form of a motion proposing a specific action, it cannot be debated. p.386*
>
> [For small groups] *Informal discussion of a subject is permitted while no motion is pending. p.488*

In formal debate, a motion and second are required to open discussion and debate. This ensures that at least two members of the body care about the matter. Small groups allow informal discussion, prior to a motion. Use care to ensure the discussion is productive. The presider ought to request a motion as soon as the group is ready for it.

Sometimes, when a proposal is perfectly clear to all present, a vote can be taken without a motion's having been introduced. Unless agreed to by unanimous consent, however, all proposed actions of a board must be approved by vote under the same rules as in other assemblies. However, someone, eventually, needs to state in clear terms what is to be voted on. What is "perfectly clear" to some members may be rather murky to others. This also relieves the secretary from having to guess just what the motion was when composing the minutes.

A second should be required.

> **ACCORDING TO ROBERT**
>
> [In formal debate] *Another member seconds the motion. p. 32*
>
> [For small groups] *Motions need not be seconded. p. 488*

While law or regulation may require a motion to be seconded, Robert's Rules of Order does not require it for small groups like councils. However, we maintain that a second ought to be required for any motion. Before a proposal takes up the group's time, there should be at least two people who want to talk about it. This is a Jurassic Parliament position that differs from Robert's Rules.

> **IN OUR EXPERIENCE**
>
> *Unnecessary debate is waste of time and resources. Preempt the frustration by ensuring that the matter is a concern of the group and that there are truly two sides to the issue to be discussed.*
> —Andrew

Members must seek recognition from the presider.

> **ACCORDING TO ROBERT**
>
> [In formal debate] *Before a member in an assembly can make a motion or speak in debate—the parliamentary name given to any form of discussion of the merits of a motion—he must obtain the floor; that is, he must be recognized by the chair as having the exclusive right to be heard at that time. p. 29*
>
> [For small groups] *Members may raise a hand instead of standing when seeking to obtain the floor. p. 487*

More than any other, this rule asserts the role of the presider in moderating the meeting. During a meeting with either formal debate or small board rules, members must seek recognition before speaking.

Members address the chair.

> **ACCORDING TO ROBERT**
>
> [In formal debate] *Members address only the chair, or address each other through the chair. p. 23; see also p. 392*
>
> [For small groups the permission to speak directly to each other is implicit in references to "informal discussion" on p. 488.]

While the small board rules allow for members to speak directly to each other, we recommend that members address all remarks to the chair as required in formal debate by large groups. This is a Jurassic Parliament position that differs from Robert's Rules. Our reasoning is that otherwise "conversations" often result, violating the rule that no one may speak a second time until everyone who wishes to do so has spoken once.

The maker of the motion may speak first.

> **ACCORDING TO ROBERT**
>
> *As soon as a member has made a motion, he resumes his seat. He will have the right to speak first in debate, if he wishes, after the chair has stated the question. p.34; see also p.379*

This rule is self-explanatory, and the same for small groups and formal debates. Whoever makes a motion speaks first after the motion has been seconded and the presider has restated it.

There is no need to alternate speakers "for" and "against."

> **ACCORDING TO ROBERT**
>
> [In formal debate] *In cases where the chair knows that persons seeking the floor have opposite opinions on the question, the chair should let the floor alternate, as far as possible, between those favoring and those opposing the measure. pp.379-380*
>
> [In small groups this permission is implicit in references to "informal discussion" on p. 488.]

In formal debate, having members alternately speak for or against a motion ensures fairness. It also ensures that debate is needed. If everyone agrees with the motion, there is no need for discussion. For small boards and councils, the round robin method can serve this function.

There is no limit to the number of speeches.

ACCORDING TO ROBERT

[In formal debate] *Unless the assembly has a special rule providing otherwise, no member can speak more than twice to the same question on the same day. pp. 388-389*

[For small groups] *There is no limit to the number of times a member can speak to a debatable question. p. 488*

In formal debate, no one may speak more than twice to a specific motion. For small boards there is no limit. However, the presider should ensure that everyone has a chance to speak once before anyone may speak twice.

There is a speech time limit.

ACCORDING TO ROBERT

In a non-legislative body or organization that has no special rule relating to the length of speeches, a member, having obtained the floor while a debatable motion is immediately pending, can speak no longer than ten minutes unless he obtains the consent of the assembly. p. 387

While Robert's Rules of Order sets a time limit of 10 minutes per speech, councils should consider a shorter limit to facilitate more effective meetings.

Members may "call the question" or move to limit debate.

ACCORDING TO ROBERT

While a debatable question is immediately pending, the allowed length or number of speeches can be reduced or increased, for that question only, by means of the subsidiary motion to Limit or Extend Limits of Debate, adopted by a two-thirds vote. p. 390

If two-thirds of those voting wish to close debate immediately, they can do so by adopting the motion for the Previous Question [Call the Question]. p. 391

[Footnote:] *Motions to close or limit debate, including motions to limit the number of times a member can speak to a question, are in order even in meetings of a small board, although occasions where they are necessary or appropriate may be rarer than in large assemblies. p. 488*

This rule is the same for formal debate and small boards. (See page 57 for details on the proper way to "call the question.")

Summary of Small Board Discussion Rules

Formal debate	Small groups
Presider does not debate.	Presider may speak in debate.
Presider does not make motions.	Presider may—but we recommend not doing so.
Must have a motion before any debate begins.	Informal discussion without a motion is allowed.
Second is required.	Second is not necessary—but we recommend it.
Members must seek recognition before speaking.	Same.
Members address remarks to the chair.	Not required—but we recommend it.
Maker of motion may speak first.	Same.
Alternate speakers "for" and "against."	Not necessary.
Limit of two speeches per member per topic.	No limit.
Speech time limit of 10 minutes.	No limit—but we recommend one be adopted.
Members may move to limit debate.	Same.

Decorum in Discussion

Robert's Rules of Order provides a framework for civilized and productive discussion and decision-making. Decorum is essential and required by Robert's Rules and common parliamentary law.

Remarks must be relevant to the topic at hand.

> **ACCORDING TO ROBERT**
>
> *In debate a member's remarks must be germane to the question before the assembly—that is, his statements must have bearing on whether the immediately pending motion should be adopted. p. 392; see also pp. xxxiv, 43*

The jargon word here is "germane." Remarks must be germane, or relevant. It is the duty of the presider to decide whether remarks are germane or not. If any two members disagree with the presider's decision, they can appeal the decision.

Members may not speak about the motives of other members.

> **ACCORDING TO ROBERT**
>
> *When a question is pending, a member can condemn the nature or likely consequences of the proposed measure in strong terms, but he must avoid personalities, and under no circumstances can he attack or question the motives of another member. p. 392; see also p. 43*

This is not about conflict of interest (although every governmental body should establish and follow a conflict of interest policy). This simply means that in ordinary discussion and debate, members are not allowed to attack or speak about the motives of their colleagues (though one may speak about one's own motives, or the motives of nonmembers).

No arguing.

There is no place for arguing at a council meeting, though vigorous—even heated—debate about controversial issues is entirely appropriate. Avoid argument by focusing on ideas, not personalities. If a council meeting becomes tense, a short recess or "stand at ease" may be in order.

"Stand at ease" often improves a meeting. The presider announces that everyone has two minutes to greet a neighbor, stand up and stretch, or refill a coffee cup. A timer is set for 120 seconds and when it goes off, the presider calls everyone back to the meeting—back "to order."

No inflammatory language (use neutral language instead).

> ### ACCORDING TO ROBERT
> *If a member disagrees with a statement by another in regard to an event that both witnessed, he cannot state in debate that the other's statement 'is false.' But he might say, 'I believe there is strong evidence that the member is mistaken.' The moment the chair hears such words as 'fraud,' 'liar,' or 'lie' used about a member in debate, he must act immediately and decisively to correct the matter and prevent its repetition.* p.392

There are as many different types of inflammatory language as there are inflamed speakers ready to spout off. An alert presider will be ready to call a halt by tapping the gavel firmly and interrupting the speaker whenever he hears remarks that are unacceptable. Members too must be ready to speak up. As always, if there is any question or objection raised to the presider's ruling, the group will decide what can be tolerated.

> ### IN OUR EXPERIENCE
> *I attended a council meeting once when a member said, "If there had been embezzlement going on, and we hadn't noticed it, we would have failed in our duty to the public." This was inflammatory. A member who fears that a crime such as embezzlement is being committed should take appropriate steps to bring it to the attention of the proper authorities. To raise the specter of crime in this casual and allusive manner, with no actual charges in mind, poisons the atmosphere and worsens relations between the elected officials and staff. No council should tolerate such remarks.* —Ann

For when you assemble a number of men to have the advantage of their joint wisdom, you inevitably assemble with those men all their prejudices, their passions, their errors of opinion, their local interests, and their selfish views.

Benjamin Franklin

A member may not speak against her own motion.

> ### ACCORDING TO ROBERT
> *In debate, the maker of a motion, while he can vote against it, is not allowed to speak against his own motion. He need not speak at all, but if he does he is obliged to take a favorable position. If he changes his mind while the motion he made is pending, he can, in effect, advise the assembly of this by asking permission to withdraw the motion.* p.393

People sometimes wonder why this rule exists in Robert's Rules. Perhaps the reason is to avoid wasting time—if a member has changed her mind as a result of arguments made by others, asking permission to withdraw the motion is simpler than continuing on to a full vote and urging that others defeat it.

A member may not explain his vote while voting.

> **ACCORDING TO ROBERT**
> *A member has no right to "explain his vote" during voting, which would be the same as debate at such a time. p. 408*

This point is self-evident and tends to save time. While we have worked with bodies who allow elected officials to give an explanation of their reasoning after the vote, sticking with Robert's Rules here is the most efficient way to process issues.

A member may not criticize a prior action of the group.

> **ACCORDING TO ROBERT**
> *In debate, a member cannot reflect adversely on any prior act of the society that is not then pending, unless a motion to reconsider, rescind, or amend it is pending, or unless he intends to conclude his remarks by making or giving notice of one of these motions. p. 393*

This rule is not well known, but is part of the general duty of loyalty that members owe to an organization. It would save a lot of hot air if groups enforced this requirement. If a member is not going to take steps to change a situation, do not discuss it at meetings.

A member must support the group.

> **ACCORDING TO ROBERT**
> *If there is an article on discipline in the bylaws, it may specify a number of offenses outside meetings for which these penalties can be imposed on a member of the organization. Frequently, such an article provides for their imposition on any member found guilty of conduct described, for example, as "tending to injure the good name of the organization, disturb its well-being, or hamper it in its work." In any society, behavior of this nature is a serious offense properly subject to disciplinary action, whether the bylaws make mention of it or not. pp. 643-644*

A member may not make statements which tend to "injure the good name of the organization, disturb its well-being, or hamper it in its work." If a member is unable to support the group, its work and its decisions, then it is time for the member to leave the group.

Sometimes the political nature of elected groups means that this rule is not enforceable. However, in the current age of individualism, it is helpful for councils and other public bodies to consider this requirement and see whether aspects of it may apply to their situation.

We believe that our public discourse would be well served if council members chose to say, when they have lost on an issue, "We have expressed our views in frank and open debate, and now it is time to move forward. I accept the will of the majority and will support the actions of this council as part of my commitment to the welfare of our community."

The willingness to engage in honest debate and lose on issues you care deeply about reaffirms your commitment to common citizenship.

Cornell W. Clayton

Round Robin Method

The simplest way to make city council meetings more efficient is to use the round robin method of discussion. In a round robin, each member of the body is given an opportunity to speak once before anyone may speak a second time, commonly by calling on the members around the table in turn. Sometimes, however, it is harder to employ this method than it seems.

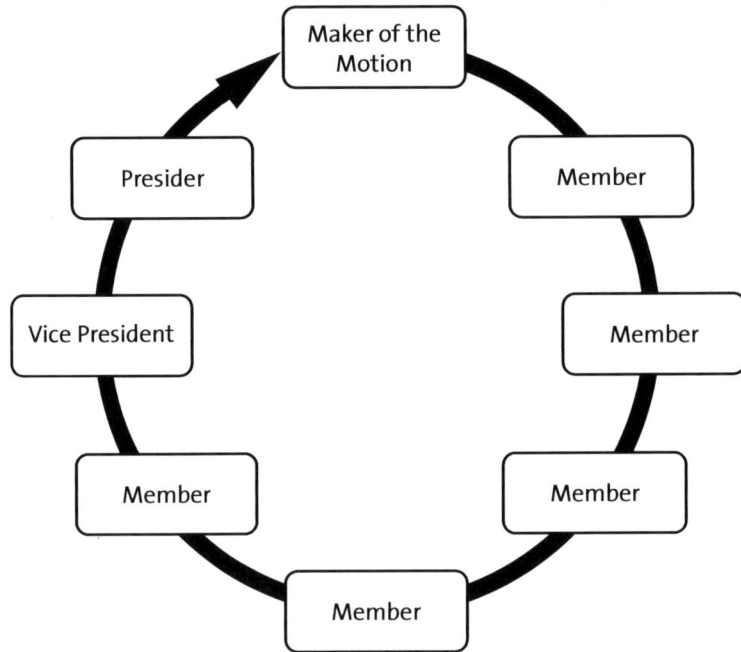

Figure 20. Round Robin

Somebody has to keep track and somebody has to be the enforcer.

Have the number two person, vice president or mayor pro tem, track speakers. This frees the presider to intervene when someone speaks out of order. This system will minimize errors often made by a presider who tries to do both.

The maker of the motion starts the debate.

Under Robert's Rules, the person who makes the motion has the right to speak first. The round robin would then move to left or right or alphabetically, depending on custom.

Everybody has to be patient.

Sometimes members are not sure what they think, or are slow to express themselves. Since council business often involves matters on which members have strong feelings, it can be a challenge to wait one's turn. Everybody involved needs to be patient for this method to succeed.

Members may pass.

It is appropriate to allow members to pass when their turn arrives, and then to offer those who passed a chance to speak at the end of the round.

It helps to vary the order.

Psychology has demonstrated the "order effect," under which those who come first in a listing often have undue influence over those who come later. If the council literally goes "around the table," alternate between moving to the left and moving to the right. If your council uses alphabetical order, start with A one time and Z the next.

You can use the popcorn style.

Under this style, there is no set order. Each person raises his hand and speaks as the spirit moves him. However, the presider or the vice-presider still tracks who has spoken, to ensure that each person gets a fair turn. If your council members are very self-disciplined, and will hold back once they've spoken the first time, people can speak up without being recognized by raising a hand.

Members must show restraint.

One of the most common violations of the round robin occurs when a member is strongly moved by a colleague's comments, and bursts out with a strong reaction. While the temptation to shout, "That's a lie!" is understandable, each member must hold back any comment until the second round.

The presider must show restraint.

Another common violation of the round robin occurs when the presider, feeling that he possesses special information of relevance to the debate, responds to each speaker. This is patently unfair, since the presider then has five or seven chances to speak to each member's single chance. Like the members, the presider must gather her thoughts in silence, and then respond to the members when her turn arrives.

The presider speaks last.

Because of the special position and weight of the presider's position, he speaks last, after all the members have spoken. This supports the neutrality of the presider's position, and also allows him to summarize the opinions expressed, a very important function—so long as it is a fair summary.

> **In Our Experience**
>
> *Having the presider speak last is not from Robert. Rather, it comes from our experience with boards, councils and other groups. Our culture is so hierarchical that we automatically defer to the leader. This violates the role of the presider as facilitator and arbiter of procedure.* —Andrew

The members must be prepared to speak up.

In the round robin, as in any gathering committed to fair use of procedure, members must be prepared to speak up when violations occur. A simple call of "point of order" should cause the presider to stop and ask, "State your point?" The member then voices her observation, and the presider either accepts the point or rules it invalid, or "not well taken." The point of order must be timely and may interrupt a speaker. (See page 59 for details on "point of order.")

The members have the final say.

If someone disagrees with the presider's decision on a point of order, any two members may appeal it. One says, "I appeal from the decision of the chair" and another says "second." The matter is then referred to the council as a whole for decision. The council itself has the final authority. Any debate on an appeal follows the same round robin pattern.

Amendments restart the round robin.

If an amendment is offered, the round robin is restarted for any debate on the amendment. Once the amendment is disposed of, the debate on the main motion picks up where it left off in the original round robin sequence. Alternatively, a group may agree to hold off on considering any amendments until everyone has had the opportunity to speak once—if agreed to, this would be a "special rule of order."

Guidelines have to be explicit.

Each council has its own culture. It is important for everyone to agree on which guidelines will be observed. These suggestions can serve as a starting point for discussion.

The city also knows that we paid a price for council wars. Those two extremes — rubber stamp and council wars — are unacceptable.

Rahm Emanuel

|

Part IV
Keeping Order

Part IV: Keeping Order

Despite all good intention and preparedness, meetings do occasionally break down. Passions can run high in the council chamber. It is vital for the presider and council members to know how to keep and restore order. Part IV includes:

- Language for both the presider and members to use when rules are broken;
- Clarity on when and how to interrupt a speaker;
- A method for ensuring fair and efficient public comment periods; and
- Concrete strategies for addressing disorder in the council chamber.

When the Rules Are Broken

A few simple phrases, and small changes in language, can quickly restore order within a council.

For the presider

When a member of the council breaks one of the rules or violates decorum, the presider should correct the offender. State the rule firmly and calmly while looking the offender in the eye:

- *Members are reminded that it is never in order to use insults in debate.*
- *Members are requested to refrain from offensive body language.*
- *Members will confine their remarks to the merits of the pending question.*

A presider may interrupt the speaker to do this, though restraint is advisable. With experience one learns when to wait, and when to leap right in.

> *You can't lead people unless you love people. You can't save people unless you serve them.... You can't navigate through life if incivility is the order. There's no other way to survive but to be kind.*
>
> Tavis Smiley

In making corrections, and while presiding in general, do not use the words "I" and "you." Speak in the "third person," not the "second person." This depersonalizes speech and keeps people focused on the business at hand rather than treating exchanges as a personal contest of wills. As an example, contrast these two sentences:

- *Hey you, you're out of order!*
- *The member is reminded that it is never in order to make personal remarks.*

Note that it is fine for members to use the pronoun "I" when speaking —and Robert's Rules expects that they will do so. However, members should also avoid the use of the word "you" whenever possible, referring to the presider as "the chair" and fellow members as "my esteemed colleague" or "the treasurer" or "my fellow council member," if they have the stomach for this type of language. If they do not, it is not worth insisting on.

For the members
If the presider fails to stop the offense, any member may speak up and say, "Point of order." The presider will rule on the point of order. If the member disagrees with the presider's ruling, any two members may appeal it, in which case the group will decide. (See page 59 for details on "point of order" and page 62 for details on "appeal.")

In the extreme case
Note that under Robert's Rules, only the group has the right to order one of its members from the room. If a member becomes belligerent or offensive, the chair may ask if one of the members would like to move that the member be directed to leave the meeting. It takes a majority vote in favor to do this. If a member is so ordered by the council and refuses to leave, the chair has the authority to direct the sergeant-at-arms to escort the member from the room.

If the presider fails to take action
If the presider fails to take a proper action, such as responding to a point of order, a member may stand up and put the motion to the group herself. The group will make the final decision by voting on the motion. Few people are aware that this is possible, but it can be very effective when a presider has lost touch with the responsibilities of his role.

When to Interrupt a Speaker

There are so many instances of rude behavior in public life today that it is not easy to know what is civil. Likewise, a false sense of not wanting to be a "troublemaker" may allow mistakes to slip by. It can be helpful to review some circumstances in which people should be interrupted.

Stop a speaker who is rude and offensive.

Speakers who make personal and insulting remarks, question motives or show discourtesy in other ways must be stopped. The chair of the meeting has the responsibility to do this, even when it means interrupting. The gavel can be helpful here—a single firm tap will often be effective.

Stop a speaker who breaks the rules.

When someone breaks the rules that the group has in place for conducting meetings, stop him. If members of the public are allowed three minutes to make their points, do not let an angry citizen continue past the time. If members of the council are required to seek recognition from the chair, do not let a council member blurt something out of turn. If the group has implemented that supremely useful rule that no one may speak a second time until everyone has spoken once, do not let an old-timer have a second chance to talk while the newly elected is waiting patiently for her turn.

Though this be madness, yet there is method in it.

Shakespeare

Make a "point of order" when a procedural mistake has been made.

When a member notices that a significant procedural mistake has been made, he should call out loudly, "Point of order." The chair has the duty to ask what the point is, and then to rule as to whether it is correct. (See page 59 for details on this motion.)

Call for a "division" when it seems that the chair may have made an error in announcing the result of a vote.

After a voice vote, the chair has the duty of announcing the results. If it seems that she may have made an error, any member may call out, "Division." The chair is then obliged to retake the vote in such a way that everyone can ascertain the results. On a city council, requesting a "roll call vote" will achieve the same result.

Under Robert's Rules, these are the most significant instances in which a speaker should be interrupted. If the city council has not adopted specific rules of procedure, it is still appropriate under common parliamentary law to use these techniques when things go awry. Sometimes we have to interrupt a speaker in order to preserve politeness and fairness for all.

And one final, and important, point. If a member, or the presiding officer, decides to let some infraction of the rules go by and not raise a point of order to correct the error (or even if no one realizes that there was an error committed at all), it will most likely be too late to do anything about it later on. Most points of order must be raised very promptly right when the infraction occurs, or else it is just too late. There are a small number of very serious errors recognized by Robert's Rules that can be corrected well after the fact, but these are rarely encountered.

Orderly Public Comment

The following guidelines establish structure and clear expectations for outside comment by nonmembers, members of the public and others. Note that different guidelines apply to public hearings, which have the sole purpose of gathering public input, and to quasi-judicial hearings.

Time considerations

Establish one or two specific periods for public comment during your meetings, in a way that is consistent with your community's expectations and customs. Set a length of time by which each period will conclude, unless the council votes to extend it. It is also important to set a time limit for each individual to speak.

Written guidelines

Provide printed copies of the guidelines and expectations for all who enter the council chamber. Review the guidelines at the beginning of each comment period if necessary, and explain that this is a time for citizens or residents to express their views in order to inform the council.

Everything has been said, but not everyone has had a chance to say it.

Carl Albert

During public comment

Require all speakers to address their remarks to the presider. This is not a discussion period. The presider should thank each speaker, whether positive or negative.

Authorize the presider to provide brief factual information, if judged appropriate, in response to public comments, or to ask the staff to provide such information. The presider must not under any circumstances enter into back-and-forth exchanges with the public.

Council members refrain from speaking during this portion of the meeting. When feasible, have staff ready to note input or questions from the public and to provide responses at a later date.

Behavioral expectations

Model courtesy and respect and require members of the public to do the same. (Use titles and honorifics—sir, ma'am, Miss Smith, Mr. Jones.) Personal attacks, insults or profanity are not allowed. Booing, hissing, cheering, clapping are not allowed.

During public comment, the presider should correct members of the public who fail to observe the guidelines. If the presider does not do this, a council member should raise a point of order. It is important for presider and members to speak in a firm, matter-of-fact manner, but not to sound overly harsh or critical. If members of the public become abusive, disruptive or violent, the presider has the authority to order them from the room.

Other suggestions

Provide clearly marked paper inviting individuals who are not heard during the public comment period due to time constraints to provide written comment for the council. Do not invite or allow public comment or questions during council discussion of its own agenda items. Be consistent in enforcing all the rules that are established.

Recognize that a governmental body must craft its requirements with care in order not to unduly limit free speech by citizens, and obtain legal review of your guidelines.

Good government obtains when those who are near are made happy and those who are far off are attracted.

Confucius

Addressing Disorder

Here is suggested language for the presider in dealing with disorder in the council chambers or at other public meetings. Key points to remember:

- All persons present at a meeting must obey the legitimate orders of the presiding officer.
- The presiding officer is the servant of the group and must obey the group's directives.
- The presiding officer has the right to order nonmembers to leave the room.
- Only the group has the right to order its members to leave the room.
- Courtesy and respect are essential for good deliberation and must be enforced.
- Do not use the words "I" and "you." Speak in the third person, as in the examples.

This material is based on *Robert's Rules of Order Newly Revised, 11th edition.* The underlying principles are taken from common parliamentary law and hold good for all public meetings. Councils should adopt additional rules of procedure for their specific circumstances.

All members—no matter how discourteous their manner or irrelevant their positions—must be dealt with seriously and with grace.

Hugh Cannon

When a council member says...	The presider can say...
Point of order!	State your point.
[If a council member can't express clearly what the point of order is...]	What rule has been broken?
Request for information *or* point of information.	State your question.
[If a council member then rambles on...]	What information does the member need to decide how to vote?
Question *or* I call the question *or* previous question	Is there a second to the call for the question?
I withdraw my motion.	Is there any objection if the member withdraws the motion?

If someone says...	The presider can say...
I'm sick of all those bleeding-heart liberal dinosaurs.	Courtesy is required at all times in our council meetings.
You're a jerk.	The rules of our council forbid the use of insults or personal attacks.
You only want to do that because you're in love with him.	Under Robert's Rules of Order it is never in order to speak about the motives of other members.
All those flying dinosaurs are lazy bums who don't pull their weight.	Our council code of procedure requires that we respect all the stakeholders in our community.
He's a liar! *[or if a member uses words like "fraud" or "embezzlement" or "baloney"...]*	Inflammatory remarks are not allowed at our meetings. The speaker will phrase his comment in a neutral manner.
!*@*@*!	Profanity is not allowed at our meetings. The speaker will kindly refrain from these improper expressions.
I think that our clerk/treasurer is on the take.	Members/citizens must refrain from making accusations of this type during a meeting, and will kindly follow our established personnel policies for dealing with concerns about possible criminal behavior.

If someone says...	The presider can say...
Hiss hiss *or* hooray hooray!	Attendees will refrain from improper expressions of sentiment.
We demand the right to speak before you vote on each motion!	Under common parliamentary law and Robert's Rules of Order, city councils have the right to determine rules for the orderly conduct of their business. We welcome citizen input during the "public comment period."
If a citizen continues to offend despite your direction...	**The presider can say...**
	Our rules of procedure prohibit behavior of this type. The attendee will kindly leave the room.
And if he doesn't leave...	The sergeant-at-arms is directed to remove the attendee from council chambers.
If a council member continues to offend despite your direction...	**The presider can say...**
	The member is reminded that the rules of our council forbid offensive behavior. The chair will ask whether any member would care to move that the offending council member be directed to leave the meeting.
If such a motion is made and a majority of the council members vote in favor...	The council member is directed to leave the room.
And if he refuses...	The sergeant-at-arms is directed to remove the council member from the chambers.
Or if the motion fails...	The motion fails, the meeting will continue.
If a riot breaks out...	**The presider can say,** This meeting is hereby adjourned.

Conclusion

Conclusion

Current habits of public discourse have coarsened our debates and made decision-making harder. By understanding the principles we have outlined, using motions wisely, adopting these guidelines and applying them consistently, councils with a majority in favor of civility and reason can create the most favorable conditions for their discussions. It is our hope that this information will help you maintain courtesy, respect and fairness in all your public meetings and make wise decisions—to the benefit of your council, your community and our society.

Appendices

Appendix A. Resources

BOOKS

Robert's Rules of Order Newly Revised, 11th edition
General Henry M. Robert
A New and Enlarged Edition by Sarah Corbin Robert, Henry M. Robert III, Daniel H. Honemann, and Thomas J. Balch, with the assistance of Daniel E. Seabold and Shmuel Gerber
DaCapo Press, a member of the Perseus Books Group Philadelphia, PA 2011

Robert's Rules of Order Newly Revised in Brief, 2nd edition
Henry M. Robert III, Daniel H. Honemann, and Thomas J. Balch, with the assistance of Daniel E. Seabold and Shmuel Gerber
DaCapo Press, a member of the Perseus Books Group Philadelphia, PA 2011

American Institute of Parliamentarians Standard Code of Parliamentary Procedure
McGraw-Hill Companies New York, NY 2012

The Standard Code of Parliamentary Procedure
Fourth edition revised by the American Institute of Parliamentarians; original edition by Alice Sturgis
McGraw-Hill Companies New York, NY 2001

Meeting Procedures: Parliamentary Law and Rules of Order for the 21st Century
James Lochrie
Scarecrow Press, Inc. Lanham, MD 2003

WEBSITES

www.jurassicparliament.com
Jurassic Parliament
The site offers a wealth of easy-to-access information in its website pages and downloads, online training, a free monthly e-newsletter, a blog and in-person training opportunities.

www.robertsrules.com
Robert's Rules Association
The site is maintained by the Robert's Rules Association, which includes descendants of General Henry M. Robert and others, and directs the revision and publication of new editions of *Robert's Rules of Order Newly Revised*. The association provides a useful list of frequently asked questions and other resources. Members of the Question and Answer Forum are generous in responding to inquiries.

www.parliamentarians.org
National Association of Parliamentarians
NAP is the largest association of parliamentarians in the U.S. The association promotes the use of Robert's Rules of Order exclusively. The site offers a wide variety of valuable materials, online training and information about in-person training events. Joining a local unit is an excellent way to become more familiar with parliamentary procedure.

Recommended: the NAP spiral-bound version of *Robert's Rules of Order Newly Revised*, 11th edition

www.aipparl.org
American Institute of Parliamentarians
AIP is the publisher of the *American Institute of Parliamentarians Standard Code of Parliamentary Procedure*. The Institute promotes the use of various parliamentary authorities. The site offers many valuable materials, online training, correspondence courses and information about in-person training events. Joining a local chapter is an excellent way to become more familiar with parliamentary procedure.

Appendix B. Motions Chart

	Rank	Second?	Debatable?	Amendable?	Vote?
PRIVILEGED MOTIONS					
Fix time to which to adjourn	13	Yes	No	Yes	Majority
Adjourn	12	Yes	No	No	Majority
Recess	11	Yes	No	Yes	Majority
Raise a question of privilege	10	No	No	No	Chair decides
Call for orders of the day	9	No	No	No	At request of one member
SUBSIDIARY MOTIONS					
Table	8	Yes	No	No	Majority
Previous question or call the question*	7	Yes	No	No	Two-thirds
Limit or extend limits of debate	6	Yes	No	Yes	Two-thirds
Postpone to a certain time	5	Yes	Yes	Yes	Majority
Refer to committee	4	Yes	Yes	Yes	Majority
Secondary amendment		Yes	Yes	No	Majority
Primary amendment		Yes	Yes	Yes	Majority
Amendment*	3	Yes	Yes	Yes	Majority
Postpone indefinitely	2	Yes	Yes	No	Majority
MAIN MOTION					
Main motion	1	Yes	Yes	Yes	Majority

* Amendment and previous question may be applied to motions higher than themselves.

INCIDENTAL MOTIONS				
	Second?	Debatable?	Amendable?	Vote?
Request for information	No	No	No	Chair responds
Point of order	No	No	No	Chair rules

BRING-BACK MOTIONS				
	Second?	Debatable?	Amendable?	Vote?
Reconsider	Yes	It depends	No	Majority
Rescind	Yes	Yes	Yes	§
Amend something previously adopted	Yes	Yes	Yes	§
Take from table	Yes	No	No	Majority

§ Majority with previous notice, two-thirds without notice, or majority of entire membership

Appendix C.
Essential Rules for Discussion and Debate for Small Boards

All references are to *Robert's Rules of Order Newly Revised, 11th edition.*
The word "implicit" means that in our view, the rule stated is assumed by Robert's Rules, or is a logical derivative of the principles on which Robert's Rules are based.

1. All members have an equal right to speak and make motions. p. 3
2. Nonmembers do not have the right to speak or to make motions. p. 648
3. One subject is discussed at a time. pp. xxxiii-xxxiv
4. One person speaks at a time. implicit
5. No interrupting. pp. 43-44, 383-384
6. Courtesy and respect are required at all times. p. 43 and implicit
7. No one may speak a second time until everyone who wishes to do so has spoken once. pp. 31, 379
8. The presider may participate in debate and make motions. p. 488 (We recommend restraint.)
9. Informal discussion without a motion is allowed. p. 488
10. A second is not needed unless law or regulation requires it. p. 488 (We recommend that a second be required.)
11. Members must seek recognition from the presider. pp. 29, 487
12. Members may speak directly to each other. p. 488 (We recommend that they do not do so, but address all remarks to the chair.)
13. The maker of the motion may speak first. p. 379
14. There is no need to alternate speakers "for" and "against." implicit
15. There is no limit to the number of speeches. p. 488

16. There is a limit of 10 minutes per speech. p. 387 (We recommend establishing a shorter limit.)
17. Members may "call the question" or move to limit debate. p. 488
18. Remarks must be relevant to the topic at hand (germane). pp. xxxiv, 43
19. Members may not speak about the motives of other members. pp. 43, 392
20. No arguing. implicit
21. No inflammatory language. p. 392, implicit
22. Courtesy and respect means:
    - No personal attacks.
    - No insults, epithets or profanity.
    - No disrespectful body language.
    - No innuendo.
    - No booing, hissing or clapping.
      pp. 43, 392, and implicit
23. A member may not speak against her own motion. p. 393
24. A member may not explain his vote while voting. p. 408
25. A member may not comment adversely on (criticize) a prior action of the group unless (a) the action is being considered for amendment or cancellation, or (b) he plans to introduce a motion to change the action at the end of his speech. p. 393
26. A member may not make statements which tend "to injure the good name of the organization, disturb its well-being, or hamper it in its work." pp. 643-644

Glossary

GLOSSARY

This glossary is intended as a user-friendly introduction to terms encountered when running meetings according to parliamentary procedure. It does not attempt to be all-inclusive or definitive.

absentee vote	vote by mail or other means in which individuals are not able to hear each other discuss an issue before voting; not allowed under Robert for boards
abstain	not to take part in a vote; under Robert, to abstain is to do nothing and abstentions are not counted
abstention	refraining from taking part in a vote
accountability hierarchy	type of organization in which members are accountable to the leader of the organization and may be hired or dismissed by him or her, e.g., business corporations or the military
action items list	running list giving actions to be taken as a result of meetings; useful in keeping all members accountable for the tasks they accept at meetings; not a part of the minutes
ad hoc committee	*see* special committee
add words	form of amendment in which words are proposed to be inserted after the body of the motion
adjourn	motion to end the meeting
adjourned meeting	meeting which is the continuation of a meeting that was started earlier
adjournment	final act at a meeting; chair may adjourn if no member is seeking recognition and there is no further business, otherwise members may move to adjourn
adopted authority	book that a group has agreed to use as its guide for procedure; synonyms: parliamentary authority, authority
adviser	person who assists the group in its activities, e.g., attorney, city manager, executive director, parliamentarian
agenda	list of specific items to be taken up in sequence at a meeting; requires a majority vote for approval; once approved, may be changed by two-thirds vote
AIP	American Institute of Parliamentarians; promotes use of several parliamentary authorities; publisher of AIPSC

AIPSC	*American Institute of Parliamentarians Standard Code of Parliamentary Procedure*; although this book is fifth in succession of the editions based on Sturgis, it is considered a new authority
amend	motion to change another motion
amend something previously adopted	motion proposing to change something the group has already adopted
amendable	motion that can be changed
amendment	content of a motion to change another motion; also the motion itself
announcement of the vote	presider's duty to announce the results of a vote after it is taken, saying "The ayes have it and the motion passes" or "The noes have it and the motion fails"
annual meeting	meeting held once a year, usually for the purpose of holding elections, adopting a budget and/or considering other matters; not customary in the civic world, since most bodies meet more frequently
appeal	motion to have the group decide whether to uphold a ruling or order of the chair
are you ready for the question?	in traditional language, question asked by the presider (1) before the group begins discussion on a motion, (2) as an invitation to continue discussion and (3) before the group votes on a motion
are you ready to vote?	alternate way of asking members in a small group if they would like to vote; recommended instead of traditional phrase, "Are you ready for the question?"; "Is there any further discussion?" also acceptable
articles of incorporation	document submitted to and approved by state government that officially creates and recognizes an organization; in the nature of an agreement between the state and the organization
assembly	formal term for a group of people who are meeting together to achieve a common purpose; synonyms: body, group
assembly, right of	right of people to gather together peaceably, protected by the First Amendment of the U.S. Constitution
association	group of people who have come together to achieve a common purpose; may refer to casual groups or formally incorporated bodies

association, right of	right of people to gather together in order to pursue a common purpose, protected by the First Amendment to the U.S. Constitution
asynchronous	not occurring at the same time, e.g., a discussion conducted by email; not allowed under Robert for decision-making on boards; *see* synchronous
authority	(1) legitimate power (2) *see* parliamentary authority
ballot	paper on which an individual's vote is indicated; may also be an electronic transmission or a counter such as a bean or a ball
ballot voting	voting by using a physical indicator, usually paper; need not be secret
board	one type of governing body; boards may differ in their authority and scope
body	general term for a group of people working together to achieve a common purpose; synonyms: assembly, group
breach	violation of the rules of order or procedure; *see* continuing breach
bring-back motion	motion that presents the assembly with a potential action on a motion previously resolved
business meeting	synonym for "regular meeting"
bylaws	agreement adopted by a body setting out how it will conduct its business; in the nature of a contract between the organization and its members; often does not have to be submitted to state government because they are considered internal
CAE	Certified Association Executive; person holding a credential offered by the American Society of Association Executives demonstrating special knowledge pertaining to association management
call for the negative	after having asked for those in favor, the presider must ask if anyone is opposed to the motion; sometimes this step is mistakenly omitted by a presider who, hearing an enthusiastic "aye," assumes that everyone is in favor
call for the orders of the day	motion demanding that the group take up the item scheduled for the particular time or point reached in the program

call for the question	in traditional terminology, this is what the presider does when she is ready to take the vote; often confused with "call the question," a motion that members can make indicating that they would like to stop debate and vote
call the question	motion to stop debate and vote on the immediately pending question; synonyms: previous question, question
call to meeting	synonym for "notice"
call to order	first act at a meeting; the presider has the duty of calling the meeting to order at the announced time or later, but not earlier
chair	(1) person holding the highest position of authority in a board of directors (2) person running a meeting; synonyms: chairman, presider, presiding officer
chairman	*see* chair
charter	document issued by a higher organization to a lower one, setting out its terms of existence
clerk	person having the duty of keeping a record of the assembly's actions and maintaining its records; may have additional duties in a given jurisdiction; synonym: secretary
closed meeting	synonym for "executive session"
commission	(1) type of governing body (2) type of committee
commit	synonym for "refer to committee"
committee	group of volunteers who have agreed to do a job defined by someone else, subordinate to the organizing body; may be permanent (standing committee) or temporary (ad hoc, select, or special committee; task force; working group)
committee of the whole	council or other governing body meeting less formally in order to study a matter; may not make final decisions while so meeting

common parliamentary law	subsection of the common law of Anglo-American society which governs the practices of voluntary associations and civic bodies; in difficult cases, different authorities may be cited in order to determine what the common parliamentary law says; *Robert's Rules of Order Newly Revised* is sometimes considered by the courts to be the best summation of the common parliamentary law
conflict of interest	personal interest that might prevent a member from voting in the best interests of the organization as a whole; Robert considers this term to apply chiefly to financial interests; bodies should establish a conflict of interest policy and must follow state law and regulation as to what constitutes a conflict of interest
consensus	mode of discussion in which members seek to find common ground and agreement rather than having to vote
consent agenda	agenda item containing a group of motions expected to be noncontroversial, which are listed together and voted on as a batch; cannot be debated; ordinarily any item can be removed from the consent agenda by request of a single member, in which case it is considered during the meeting and may be debated; synonym: consent calendar
consent calendar	synonym for "consent agenda"
constitution	(1) *see* U.S. Constitution (2) *see* constitution and bylaws
constitution and bylaws	in earlier times many voluntary organizations had both a constitution and bylaws, with the constitution less detailed and more difficult to change; this is now considered to be confusing, and it is recommended that organizations adopt one document, the bylaws, covering all the various points needed
continuing breach	violation of the rules of order so serious that members' fundamental rights have been violated; in this rare case, point of order may be raised even if not timely, e.g., a motion has been passed that conflicts with the bylaws
conversation	type of informal discussion in which people are free to interrupt one another, speak when they feel like it or speak several times in a row; not recommended as the mode for small group meetings and not allowed in formal assemblies

council	type of board; in this book used to indicate elected individuals exercising legislative authority for a city, county, special district or other local government
counted vote	vote in which the number of "ayes" and "noes" is counted by the presider and recorded in the minutes
courtesy	politeness and respect for others; essential to effective discussion
COW	Committee of the Whole
crosstalk	two members speaking directly to one another, rather than addressing their remarks to the chair
custom	method of functioning which is not included in the rules of procedure or otherwise written down, but has become usual through long usage; has some standing in parliamentary procedure but is lowest of all, and must yield if it violates a fundamental principle of parliamentary law or any adopted rules
debatable	motion that can be discussed
debate	*see* formal debate
decorum	order, courtesy and respect in carrying out the business of the body
deliberation	synonym for "discussion"
dilatory	motion that wastes the group's time; presider has duty not to allow discussion on dilatory motions; synonym: frivolous
discussion	time in which members consider the issue at hand in order to determine what action to take; synonyms: debate, deliberation
division	term said loudly by member who believes there is some question as to how a voice vote was called by the presider; presider must immediately take vote again by a different method so the outcome can be clearly ascertained
draft agenda	agenda as prepared before the meeting; not final until accepted by group
draft minutes	minutes as prepared by secretary; not final until approved by group; if distributed should be clearly marked as "draft"; should not be distributed beyond membership
duties of members	members must follow the rules of procedure, obey the legitimate orders of the presiding officer and support the group; they have other duties as well

elected official	individual who has been chosen by voters to fulfill a particular office
electronic voting	may be allowable if law, regulations and bylaws permit; now sometimes allowed for membership organizations but in general not for boards of directors or civic bodies
email voting	*see* voting by email
emergency meeting	meeting held in urgent situation; sometimes rules allow for waiver of the notice requirements; if not properly called, or if a quorum not present, persons present may be liable for actions taken should the full body fail to ratify those actions at a regular meeting
en bloc	term used when a group of motions are voted on all at once, as a batch, e.g., motion to adopt a consent agenda (French)
ex officio member	individual who holds membership in a given body because of his position, rather than because he has been elected to the body; ordinarily a full voting member unless rules specify otherwise
ex parte	meeting individually, outside the meeting itself, with persons concerned in a quasi-judicial matter (Latin)
executive session	meeting held with only members and, perhaps, selected staff or guests in attendance; contents must be held confidential; synonyms: closed meeting, in camera, secret meeting
extend debate	motion to allow more time for discussion
federal law and regulation	federal law and regulation, insofar as it exists with reference to civic bodies, has higher standing than state law and regulation; acts of a body must conform to it
fix time to which to adjourn	motion to resume the current meeting at a proposed future time; adopting the motion does not stop, or adjourn, the current meeting
flow of authority	system embodied in Robert's Rules whereby the group adopts its rules and the presider enforces the rules to serve the group, but if any question arises, the group decides and the presider accepts the group's ruling; basis of democracy
formal debate	discussion conducted according to certain rules given in Robert, e.g., the presiding officer does not participate in debate, each member may speak twice for up to 10 minutes at a time, etc.

formality	a more old-fashioned way of respectful interaction; recommended; a modest degree of formality helps separate personalities from ideas and improves deliberation by the body; e.g., "Madam Chairman, it seems that this motion is out of order," rather than "Ann, he's nutty to make that proposal"
friendly amendment	form of amendment that the maker believes will improve a motion or make it more likely to pass; often processed improperly
frivolous	synonym for "dilatory"
fundamental principle	principle that is integral to parliamentary law; Robert lists several examples
general consent	synonym for "unanimous consent"
germane	relevant; amendments must be germane to the main motion and remarks must be germane to the subject being discussed; an amendment can reverse the intent of a motion and still be germane
good of the order	old-fashioned term, often included as an agenda item towards the end of the meeting as an opportunity for members to make general remarks commending, censuring or suggesting actions that the body might wish to undertake
governing body	group of people who have collectively assumed legal and moral responsibility for directing an organization; synonym: board
group	general term for several people working together to achieve a common purpose; synonyms: assembly, body
guest	synonym for "nonmember"
half plus one	incorrectly but often used to indicate "majority," but the term is deprecated since one cannot have a fraction of a person voting; "more than half" or "more than 50%" is a better definition of "majority"
hereby	useful term to add weight to an official action; may be used by presider, e.g., "This meeting is hereby called to order," or in text of motion, e.g., "This body hereby declares that personal attacks are prohibited"
hostile amendment	form of amendment intended to make a motion less likely to pass or to negate its intent
hypothetical question	question which does not pertain to the actual situation; presider is not obliged to answer hypothetical questions

if there is no objection	synonym for "without objection"
improper language	rude or offensive language; not permitted under Robert; body should also adopt, with legal advice, rules of procedure to handle
in camera	synonym for "executive session" (Latin)
in good standing	entitled to participate according to the bylaws and/or rules of the organization
in order	correct
incidental main motion	main motion that does not introduce a new proposal, e.g., motion to amend something previously adopted
incidental motions	motions that do not directly pertain to the motion under consideration
inflammatory language	language tending to excite emotion and confuse discussion; not allowed under Robert; e.g., "That's a lie" or the word "fraud"
inquorate	not having a quorum present
insert words	form of amendment in which words are proposed to be inserted within the body of the motion
is there any further discussion?	alternate way of asking members in a small board if they would like to vote; recommended instead of traditional phrase, "Are you ready for the question?"; "Are you ready to vote?" also acceptable
kindly	useful term for presider to soften his orders, presenting them as if they were requests; e.g., "Members will kindly refrain from using offensive language"
law	*see* common parliamentary law
lay on the table	synonym for "table"
limit debate	motion to shorten time allowed for discussion
mail vote	form of absentee vote in which ballots are distributed and collected via postal mail; not allowed for boards or civic bodies
main motion	proposal for a group to take up a new action
majority	more than 50%; more than half
majority of entire membership	more than half of the full membership of the body
majority vote	vote in which more than half of those participating vote in favor

maker	person who first proposes a motion; sometimes mistakenly assumed to "own" the motion—once a motion has been made, seconded and stated by the chair, the maker has right to speak first in its favor, but beyond that, she has merely the same rights as all other members
mayor	person holding highest office in a city; may be elected in own right or elected from among the members of a city council
meeting	gathering of a group of people to conduct their business
meeting by telephone	*see* telephonic meeting
minority	less than half; Robert is very concerned to protect the rights of the minority
minutes	official record of actions taken by a body; draft prepared by the clerk or secretary, but not final until approved by group, which has right to make corrections
motion	proposal made by a member for a group to take action
motions list	list of all motions passed by a body; useful in keeping members aware of previous actions
motive	personal intention; discussion of members' motives, other than possible conflict of interest issues, is not allowed during debate
NAP	National Association of Parliamentarians; promotes use of *Robert's Rules of Order Newly Revised* exclusively
negative vote	voting against a motion; after calling for those in favor, presider must call for the negative; it is important that members be ready to vote against a proposal if they disagree with it, and not hold back from fear of seeming disagreeable
new business	time in a meeting during which business that has not yet been taken up may be considered by a body
nonmember	person who does not belong to the group (including staff, advisers and members of the public); has no privileges other than those granted by law, regulation or the group; synonym: guest
not well taken	incorrect

notice	notification to members and the public that a meeting is to be held; all members have the right to adequate and timely notice; inadequate notice has been found to invalidate business conducted at a meeting; synonym: call to meeting
objection	term used by members when they do not wish to proceed by unanimous consent; no need to obtain recognition before saying "objection"; if there is objection, presider immediately proceeds to process the motion or matter in the usual way
officer	an individual charged with particular responsibilities in running or serving a group
old business	outdated term for "unfinished business"
open meeting	meeting open to anyone who wishes to attend; many states have "open meeting acts" that specify exactly what this means
order of business	customary sequence of events at a meeting; the agenda is based on the organization's order of business as provided in its adopted authority
order of chair	directive by presider that, if legitimate, must be obeyed by everyone present at a meeting; may be appealed by any two members of the group, with the group being the final authority; *see* ruling by chair
orders of the day	schedule of items showing what should be taken up when
ordinance	law passed by a municipality
out of order	incorrect
parliamentarian	adviser to the chair and assembly who is knowledgeable about the rules of procedure; may be a member or guest
parliamentary authority	book that a group has agreed to use as its guide for procedure; synonyms: authority, adopted authority
parliamentary inquiry	request asking for information about an aspect of parliamentary procedure relevant to the current situation
parliamentary law	(1) *see* common parliamentary law (2) book written by Henry Martyn Robert, considered to be one of the leading sources for difficult questions going beyond Robert's Rules of Order

parliamentary procedure	system of running meetings derived from common parliamentary law and explicated in *Robert's Rules of Order Newly Revised* and other authorities
pending motion	motion being considered at the moment; the next motion to be taken up
permanent committee	*see* committee
point of clarification	made-up term often used by someone who wants to speak out of turn in order to provide information that she judges to be relevant; member should be gently directed to provide the information when her turn next arrives during debate
point of general privilege	motion pertaining to rights of the entire body
point of information	older term, now considered incorrect, meaning "request for information"; sometimes misused to provide information rather than to ask a question
point of order	motion or assertion claiming that a mistake has been made
point of personal privilege	motion pertaining to the rights of the speaker
policy	guidelines established by a body to conduct its business, lower in rank than the bylaws; generally pertains to the body's functioning in areas other than procedure
postpone	*see* "postpone to a definite time" and "postpone indefinitely"
postpone indefinitely	motion to kill a motion without actually voting against it
postpone to a definite time	motion to stop considering a motion at the meeting under way and take it up at a future time or meeting
precedence of motions	system established in common law, Robert's Rules of Order and other authorities by which certain motions have a number or rank attached to them; while a motion is pending, motions with a higher rank may be made, but motions with a lower rank are out of order (*see* Appendix B)
president	person holding the highest office in an organization
presider	*see* chair
presiding officer	*see* chair

previous notice	notice given in advance that one intends to present a motion at a future meeting; may be done orally, or by including the item in a call to the meeting distributed in advance
previous question	synonym for "call the question"
primary amendment	amendment to a main motion
privilege	rights of the assembly or the individual
privileged motion	motions 9-13 in the Motions Chart (Appendix B) relating to the rights or privileges of the organization or members, rather than to particular items of business
pro tem	synonym for "pro tempore"
pro tempore	serving in an office which one does not regularly hold, usually for a short interval; synonyms: pro tem, temporary (Latin)
proclamation	formal statement by an authority or a civic body, usually announcing a positive action of some kind, such as an honor or a special day, week or month
proxy	(1) the right to vote on another person's behalf, given by a member to his proxyholder; not allowed in boards and civic bodies (2) form given by member to proxyholder indicating that the proxyholder has the right to vote on behalf of the other person, and sometimes how she should vote
PRP	Professional Registered Parliamentarian; person holding credential offered by NAP who has demonstrated knowledge of parliamentary procedure and skills as parliamentarian and presiding officer
public comment	period of time during a meeting of a civic body dedicated to receiving input from members of the public; the requirements of state law may determine aspects of this agenda item
public hearing	meeting held for the purpose of learning the views of members of the public
public record	documents created by a governmental body that must be disclosed to members of the public upon request
quasi-judicial hearing	meeting during which council functions as a judicial body, rather than as a legislative one

question	(1) general term in parliamentary procedure for the subject or motion under consideration (2) synonym for "call the question"
quorate	having a quorum present
quorum	minimum number of voting members who must be present for business to be done; if not otherwise specified, a majority of the membership
raise a question of privilege	motion bringing up a matter pertaining to the rights of the assembly or an individual
ratify	(1) to confirm decisions previously taken that were in some way improperly made, e.g., a quorum was not present (2) to endorse actions taken by another body
recess	motion to take a short break
recognition	authorization of the chair that an individual member or other person may speak; Robert has rules determining who is entitled to be recognized and in what order
reconsider	one of the "bring-back" motions that proposes to take up something again that the group had previously disposed of
refer to committee	motion to send a main motion (and any other motions pertaining to it) to a committee; synonym: commit
regular meeting	ordinary scheduled meeting of a body; synonyms: business meeting, meeting
renew	to reintroduce a previously defeated motion; most defeated motions can be "renewed" at any future meeting
request for information	motion made when a member needs certain urgent information, relevant to the debate, in order to decide how to vote; now considered to be a more correct term than "point of information"
rescind	one of the "bring-back" motions that proposes to cancel out something that the group has already adopted
resolution	more formal type of motion, usually containing introductory clauses beginning with "Whereas" that give reasons for the action, and concluding with the clause "Now therefore be it resolved that…"; Robert has specific rules about the order in which the portions of a resolution are processed

respectfully submitted	a phrase formerly used by the secretary or other author of a report above the signature; now considered outmoded
rights of members	in general members have the right to be notified of meetings in a timely manner; to participate in discussion; to make motions and vote, and to serve as officers; other rights may be included in the bylaws
Robert	(1) Henry Martyn Robert, 1827 – 1923, the original author of Robert's Rules of Order; began his career in the U.S. Army Corps of Engineers and concluded it as a general (2) short name for *Robert's Rules of Order Newly Revised*, which may also be cited as RONR
roll call	calling out the name of each member in order to determine who is present
roll call voting	method of voting by which the clerk or secretary calls the name of each member, who answers "aye" or "no"; may also be conducted by electronic means if a body has the equipment; votes must be recorded in the minutes
RONR	acronym for *Robert's Rules of Order Newly Revised*
round robin	useful form of discussion in which each member of a body is invited to speak in turn, with everyone else, including the presider, refraining from interruption or comment until their proper turn arrives
rules	the basis of democratic action; without mutually accepted rules, force prevails
rules of procedure	system of organizing meetings so that they are orderly, fair and as efficient as possible
ruling by chair	decision by the presider on a question of procedure; if legitimate, must be obeyed by everyone present at a meeting; may be appealed by any two members of the group, with the group being the final authority; *see* order of chair
same sign	obsolete and confusing method of calling for the negative vote; better to say, "All those opposed say 'no'"
second	to say the word "second" aloud, thereby indicating that one wishes to have a motion discussed by the group; *see also* seconder of motion
secondary amendment	amendment to a primary amendment

seconder of motion	person who seconds the motion; the seconder is sometimes mistakenly considered to have "ownership rights" in the motion, but once a motion has been made, seconded and stated by the chair, the seconder has merely the same rights as all other members
secret ballots	pieces of paper that are processed in such a way that the identity of each voter is concealed from those counting the vote; may also be a protected electronic transmission
secret meeting	synonym for "executive session"
secret vote	vote in which individual persons cannot be linked with the vote cast; usually not used in civic meetings because of open meeting requirements for transparency
secretary	person having the duty of keeping a record of the assembly's actions and maintaining its records; may have other duties; synonym: clerk
select committee	*see* special committee
sergeant-at-arms	officer with the duty of maintaining order at the assembly's meetings
show of hands	method of voting in which first those in favor raise a hand, then those opposed; presider must ask people to keep a hand up long enough either to verify which side has the majority, or to count the votes
sidebar conversation	members whispering to each other during a meeting
simple majority	obsolete term meaning "majority"
small board	defined by Robert as up to about 12 people
small board rules	rules provided in *Robert's Rules of Order Newly Revised, 11th edition*, for small boards and committees; Jurassic Parliament recommends that some of them be modified
special committee	committee created for a particular purpose that goes out of existence once its duties are complete; synonyms: ad hoc committee, select committee, task force, working group
special rules of order	rules that a body adopts in addition to or superseding the rules contained in its adopted parliamentary authority

staff	employees of a city or other organization; ordinarily not members of the governing body, but may offer advice and consultation; at a meeting, the staff have the status of guests of the assembly
stand at ease	short period of time (about two minutes) during which members are released from the obligation to attend to the business of the body, while remaining in place
Standard Code	*see* TSC and AIPSC
standing	entitlement to participate
standing committee	ongoing, permanent committee
standing rules	rules pertaining to the administrative functioning of an organization
state law and regulation	state law and regulation set the foundation for most organized bodies in the United States; bylaws, rules and regulations adopted must conform to the laws and regulations of the state in which the body exists or is incorporated
strike out and insert words	form of amendment in which it is proposed that certain words be deleted and others inserted in their place
strike out words	form of amendment in which it is proposed that certain words be deleted
strong mayor	mayor who is elected to her position independently of the council; has administrative, leadership and ceremonial responsibilities
study session	synonym for "work session"
Sturgis	(1) Alice Sturgis, 1885 – 1974, original author of *The Standard Code of Parliamentary Procedure* (2) short name for *The Standard Code of Parliamentary Procedure*
subsidiary motion	motions 2-8 in the Motions Chart (Appendix B), used to change or process a main motion
substitute	form of amendment in which new language is proposed to replace the currently existing language
supermajority vote	any requirement for passage of a motion greater than a majority vote
suspend the rules	motion to do something that is contrary to the rules of order
synchronous	occurring at the same time; Robert requires that a meeting be synchronous; *see* asynchronous

table	motion enabling a body to put a motion aside while some other business is conducted; often misused by members wishing to kill a motion without voting on it—the correct motion for this purpose is to "postpone indefinitely"
take from the table	motion enabling a body to resume consideration of a motion that was previously tabled
task force	*see* special committee
telephonic meetings	if laws, regulation and bylaws permit, meetings may be conducted by telephone provided that each member can hear and be heard; these are "synchronous" meetings; video and network conferencing are also possible
teller	person who counts votes
temporary committee	*see* committee
tertiary amendment	does not exist; once a primary and secondary amendment have been made, no further amendment is possible until they are resolved
treasurer	officer charged with handling finances; same individual should not serve as both treasurer and bookkeeper
TSC	*The Standard Code of Parliamentary Procedure*, the first version of which was written by Alice Sturgis; synonyms: Standard Code, Sturgis
two-thirds majority	incorrect term meaning "two-thirds vote"
two-thirds vote	vote requiring that at least two-thirds vote in favor for passage
U.S. Constitution	highest authority governing actions of an assembly, though seldom invoked as a specific reference
unanimous consent	method of voting in which the presider asks, "Are there any objections?"; members who agree with the proposed action say nothing, and their silence means consent; synonym: general consent
unanimous written consent in lieu of a meeting	method of voting under which, if authorized by law, regulation and bylaws, all members sign a written consent to an action instead of meeting in person to vote; written consents must be filed with the minutes; invalid if any member fails to sign; legal opinions differ as to whether an emailed consent meets the requirements of this method

unfinished business	business carried over from a previous meeting by very specific means
very well	useful phrase presider can use to move group calmly on to the next item of business
vice-chair	second-in-command to the chair
vice-president	second-in-command to the president
viva voce	synonym for "voice voting" (Latin)
voice voting	method of voting in which members use their voices, saying "aye" or "no"
voluntary association	type of organization in which members have joined of their own accord and are all of equal rank, with equal rights, privileges and obligations
vote	process of decision-making; there are several different methods of voting, some not covered in this book
voting by email	ordinarily boards and civic bodies are not allowed to vote by email because the vote is asynchronous and absentee; Robert considers that oral argument and exchange of views is critical to valid decision-making
weak mayor	mayor who is elected by a city council from among its members, not in her own right
well taken	correct
whereas	useful term for listing the reasons behind an action and giving weight to a motion; a resolution often starts with several "Whereas" clauses
without objection	useful phrase for presider to make a suggestion to the group, while acknowledging that the group is the final authority; synonym: If there is no objection
work session	meeting of an elected body to review subject(s) in depth, hear from staff and discuss alternatives; usually no vote may be taken; is ordinarily a public meeting; synonym: study session
working group	*see* special committee

Index

INDEX

Afterword

This body of knowledge is continuously evolving, and we welcome your participation as we continue to develop it. What feedback do you have for us? What works for you in this book and what doesn't? What other topics would you like to see covered in our publications?

We invite our readers to connect with us in any or all of the following ways:

- Visit our website, www.jurassicparliament.com

- Read our blog, "Robert's Rules in Real Life"

- Follow us on Twitter @MeetingMastery

- Like us on Facebook, www.facebook.com/JurassicParliament

- Email us at info@jurassicparliament.com

- Write us a letter at 603 Stewart St., Suite 610
  Seattle WA 98101 USA

- Give us a call at 206-542-8422 (Pacific Time)

Thank you for your interest and support. We look forward to being in touch.

13420585R00091

Printed in Great Britain
by Amazon